I Am A Gift

DISCOVERING THE BEAUTY OF BIBLICAL WOMANHOOD

TINA WILSON TAYLOR

Cover Design Tina Taylor

Cover Photo Canva.org

I AM A GIFT
Copyright © 2020 by Gratiana (Tina) Wilson Taylor
Conyers, GA 30094
tinatayloronline.com

ISBN 978-1-7351357-1-7 (paperback)
ASIN B089KQL6QG (ebook)
Names: Taylor, Tina Wilson, 1980-author
Title: I Am A Gift: Discovering the True Beauty of Womanhood/ Tina Wilson Taylor
Other titles: I Am A Gift
Description: Conyers, GA
Identifiers: 978-1-7351357-1-7 (pbk) B089KQL6QG (ebook)
Subjects: Nonfiction > Religion > Christian Life Nonfiction >Family & Relationships > Marriage and Long-Term Relationships.

Mom,
You are the example of biblical
womanhood. Thank you for helping
me find my way.

Corey,
Thank you for your patience as
I continue to grow.

Eden, Joy, and Erin
May your journey to womanhood end
in the same place of all the godly women
before you.

Contents

Why Do We Feel This Way?

Have you ever reached the end of your day and realized everything you did was for someone other than yourself? Are you ever confused about your role and responsibilities only to become frustrated when they do not meet others' expectations? Do you find that you often overextend yourself by saying, "Yes," when you want to say, "No?"

Maybe you're just tired of being told to "submit" and you're angry at how the world – or even the church – treats you simply because you're a woman? After many self-sacrificing experiences, I understand if you have ever thought – *It is not fair being a woman.*

Whether you have been shamed into believing your opinion does not matter or objectified and used because of your body, your looks, or your position, you are not alone. Maybe you have been rejected and abused by so many people, and you now find it tough to consider that you have value and worth. No matter where you are in your expression of being a woman, you do not have to stay there.

I'm guessing you picked up this book because you are interested in how to live better, healthier, and happier. Maybe someone in your life shared this book with you because it highlights an answer to a problem you have shared with them. Regardless of the reasons, you are here looking for something.

If any of this describes you, please know that I can relate to you and what you are feeling. I have been there, and I understand the challenges of everyday life as a woman. There is so much to do and so little time. No matter what I did, it seemed my list continued to grow, and my needs were pushed further to the bottom. I was coasting through life, hitting all the cultural milestones set for women: an education, marriage, and childbirth. I believe I hit a wall at age 33 when I deliberately began looking at my life to assess how things were going. I realized I was caring for everyone except myself. I considered the preferences of my husband, my child, my family, my clients, and my community, all while neglecting my own heart. By age 36, I was unhappy with my terrific life. I was living for others while losing myself, and there seemed to be little reciprocity.

Just like you, acknowledging I was not happy was not enough to change my life. Oh no! This continued for another two years because I just did not know how to stop living for others. I wanted to quit, runaway, and tell everyone, "No, I am not available." But there was a small voice within me asking, *Who did I want to take my place?* I could not think of anyone else I wanted to care for my husband, children, clients, or my community. I did not want anyone else to do it. I just did not know how to do it all.

I needed to make a change. I had to do something different. It seemed I was fighting against myself every day. What I desired to do was not reflected in my behaviors. Acknowledging that my desires and actions were so different only led me to depression and despair. These feelings remained with me for a long time until I truly embraced the beauty of being a woman. It was at this place in my journey when I decided to rediscover the purpose of a woman. When my perception and attitude changed, the way I approached my list changed too. After wrestling with myself and the truth, I understood why I am here and the beauty of my purpose. While the list is still present, I am convinced that God designed the woman – you and me – as a gift. A precious, cherished, and priceless gift.

I am not asking you to take a journey I have not started myself. I know that changing your perception about womanhood will impact the way you behave in your relationships as a wife, a mother, a daughter, a sister, and a friend. Knowing your design will give you a greater sense of value and worth. That confidence shows up in your relationships where you are now free to be uniquely you, a gift in all your different circles.

Our Road Map

As you read this book, you will be guided to identify your thoughts about womanhood and how you formed this mental picture of what it means to be a woman. Together we can identify the sources we often use to measure ourselves and replace them with the truth of how we were created. We will seek out what God had in mind when He created woman and embrace His design as our standard in living out this life. We will clarify that while we are a gift that is given to others, we are also human and made to rest. Maybe it has been so long that you have forgotten what it is like to take time to yourself. Yep, by the end of this book, you can have less guilt about saying "NO" and taking a nap every now and then. All the while, you can still care for the things and people who matter the most to you.

In this book I want to help you:

- realize your worth as a woman.
- understand your relationship with Christ.
- embrace your calling as a treasured aid, helper, and champion.
- receive empowerment that calls you to action.
- experience the joy that results from living your divine purpose.
- love others more as you realize how very much you are loved.
- improve your relationships as you better understand who you are and why you are here.
- live your purpose as a single, married, divorced, or widowed woman.

Our Travel Companions

Celebrating the creation of woman requires understanding the purpose and intent of our innate qualities. While no two women are alike, our goals and mission are the same across generations and cultures. My purpose in writing this book is to invite you to explore the thoughts and behaviors associated with womanhood. Secondary to this goal is to create a movement to redefine womanhood, starting with you, your community, and then the world. This will be accomplished as you share this book with other women.

I recommend that you create a space where you and other women can share experiences to help create your expression of womanhood. In this space, there is intentional reflection and communication about life experiences that have molded current perceptions and behaviors. We will journey together through culture, Scripture, and personal experiences to help arrive at a place of healing and wholeness in understanding why we were created.

As a licensed professional counselor, I understand there is no one answer for every life situation. As a follower of Jesus Christ, I do believe the goal of carrying one another's burdens is essential in reaching solutions for all of us. Through the process of sharing our comforts and challenges in our decision making, we can appreciate and celebrate our differences. The housewife and the heroine can stand and admire one another for the expression of womanhood they each display.

I will share a few of my experiences, even though I recognize my experiences are unique to me. However, the emotions I have felt are common to all women. How fear, resentment, self-doubt, loneliness, and the like show up in life varies between you and me. Your story may be about rejection and another woman's story might be about rape and abuse. We all have the same need to heal and rid ourselves of the stain that keeps us from bearing the beautiful image of God in our lives.

Throughout this book, I will share how I wrestled with various views on the purpose and design of a woman. I will give you opportunities to reflect on your thoughts and behaviors. You, too, may find that your beliefs and behaviors as a woman clash. I realize my goal may create upheaval to your thoughts, feelings, and lifestyle. This is not to create confusion. I believe if you fully engage in this process, you will experience clarity and transformation. You will identify the truth and learn how to embrace and express the gift within you. You will become sure about who you are and why you are here. With a deep-seated conviction of who you are, you will have a more significant impact on those around you!

I am hoping what I share will make life easier and more enjoyable for you as a woman. I am sharing what I believe is the purpose of God in designing you and me. You may or may not have a relationship with Jesus Christ. Admittedly, if you do not have a relationship with Christ or currently struggle with relating to Him, reading this book will create some friction. To get the most out of this book, consider starting with "Knowing Your Creator" on page 143 to learn more about Christ and how to receive Him as your Savior. After that, return to the beginning of the book as I believe my expression of these ideas will encourage you to understand that you are a gift to others. And the *gift* that you are has significant value.

Additionally, I want to help with the struggles you might be experiencing in your relationships with others. Very real pain and wounds are caused by the people we love or the people who promised to love us. Pain is a challenge to embracing the truth. I'm committed to helping you move through the pain and reach a place of purpose, beginning with believing that *you are still a gift.* No matter your experiences and despite the people who did not show up in your life or the people who left your life, you are valuable. If you are still dealing with the pain of a relationship, I have written something special for you on page 145 called "Reclaiming the Lost Gift." Consider starting there before you begin the next chapter.

My prayer is that you will come away from this book with a stronger desire to nurture the people in your life. I am not promising it will be without sweat or struggle. But I do guarantee you will experience joy as you realize why you were designed, and live out your divine purpose. May you be convinced and confident to declare proudly: "I AM A GIFT!"

"Don't let anyone dim your light, it was God-given."

F. Nicole Williams

Wife, Mother, Superhero

1

How Did We Get Here?

M any of us have the same daily routines. There may be some slight differences, but most days, we are not surprised by the day's events. However, have you ever experienced a day when you looked up from your routine and realized you are not quite where you thought you would be? You completed your education and settled into the profession of your dreams, yet you are still not doing the work you thought you would be doing. Maybe you are doing exactly what you thought you would, but somehow you are less happy than you thought you would be. What about your relationships? You may have dated your husband for a long time before marrying and thought you knew him, but when you look at your marriage today, it is not quite what you thought it would be. You wonder, *How did I get here?*

Every woman has had those moments when she realizes what she envisioned does not match the reality of how she is living. We all call those moments "waking up and smelling the roses," discontentment, disillusionment, or unmet goals. Regardless of what you call it, the feeling is the same. We feel deceived or that we have missed something along the way. We start to wonder where we took a wrong turn and if we can ever get back to what we imagined or dreamed. We may even ask ourselves, *What happened? Why did this happen?* and *How can I keep it from happening again?*

If this is true about many different situations in life, it too, can be relevant when we look at our lives as women. When we were teenagers, I'm sure we all thought about what it would be like as an adult woman. Maybe we thought about where we would live or if we would marry and have children. We probably thought about the profession we would choose and how we would financially care for ourselves. But, did we ever wonder how we would live in relation to others? I never thought about the feelings or attitudes of the women I saw on television or in magazines. They always looked happy, and the subtle message was that if I did what they did, I, too, would be a happy woman. So now that we are looking beyond our routines, it becomes clear how the image of womanhood has arrived at where it is today.

Media Messages

Every generation of women was given intentional messages and themes about womanhood communicated by the media. I grew up in the '80s and '90s. This was a time when it was all about having fun. Individualism was encouraged while still valuing the community. My youth was filled with media messages on living drug-free and practicing safe sex. Movies, television commercials, music, and magazine ads were all about experiencing all the life you could, but doing it safely.

Another message the media taught me was that men and women are the same. Women did not need men to be successful in the world and were encouraged to live a life independent of a man. Before long, I was quoting lines like "I don't need a man" and singing "I'm every woman."

While the media messages about womanhood bombarded me, I still held the values and views of my Christian household. My upbringing taught me about the creation of mankind to include the purpose and design for both men and women. I understood that God created man and woman to have dominion over the earth. I understood there was an order of care, responsibility, and authority God created for mankind: God cared for the man; the man cared for the woman. The response to this order was respect. The woman respected the man; the man had a fervent respect for God. I believed this to be true. Yet, I had also adopted the viewpoint that men and women could live independently of one another. It was not until later in life that these two beliefs collided. The collision created mental and emotional chaos that I continue to work to overcome.

I bet the same is true for you too. What you saw growing up without a doubt impacts how you live your life today. In times past, both the media and Christendom gave messages that considered the woman as the "other." She was domestic support, to be seen and not considered. She was incapable of making decisions because of her emotional sensitivity. Her worth was found only in her relationship with a man and the family unit. She was devalued, often disregarded, disrespected, and worse, put to death.[1] We see the mistreatment of women in both developing and developed countries where they are often exploited for their bodies in magazine ads and films. In many countries, the bodies of women are considered the property of a man, and the women experience all forms of physical and sexual violence. Depending on where you live, women are treated as sexual goddesses or sexual slaves.

This most certainly is not why women were created, nor what they deserve. A great number of women's movements have helped change these ideas. Yet, the work is not done as we have landed in a place that still is not beneficial for you or me.

Within the last 70 years, women have been encouraged to pave a new path for themselves alone. In developed countries, women are praised for the ability to dominate independently of men, children, and other women. They are encouraged to adopt an individualistic mindset, which is contrary to her creation. The messages in the media today claim to liberate women. Unfortunately, what is proposed may seem fitting for women, but it is not beneficial to humanity.

The picture of womanhood is eroding as the woman seeks to become more independent of others when she was created to foster relationships intertwined with others. In the name of uplifting women, many media campaigns seek to change a woman's design. The lure of the message is that being an independent woman is the pinnacle of womanhood. This is a far cry from the origins of womanhood but instead emulates what society has defined as manhood. Society celebrates womanhood by recommending we behave like a man. The current projection of womanhood is only a representation of what women lack from times past, not what we have gained in the present.

> *To celebrate being a woman, it is recommended she behave like a man.*

Over time, women and men have attempted to change this idea. The efforts have become extreme as the message today is that women are not only independent of men, but also are driven to be better than men. The media claims to "celebrate" the rise of women in power. Yet, dominating men is the recommendation of how women achieve their power. You can see this idea demonstrated through seduction and the threat of being called a misogynist.

Ironically, the domination of a man still requires his acceptance. Myles Monroe said it best in his book, *The Power and Purpose of a Woman*. In essence, he emphasizes that the woman is born with innate rights. When the woman asks the man for permission to rule then she is implying he possesses her rights. When women realize that we already have everything we need within Jesus Christ to fulfill our purpose, we will behave differently and thereby interact with others differently.

> "There is a significant difference between demanding one's rights from someone and displaying the rights one already possesses… If we understand that the women's position and rights in the world are inherent, it is going to change our approach to solving her plight worldwide."[2]

If we take into consideration the thought above, the rise of women does not begin with forcing men to change in as much as it starts with a change within women. How can we, as women, display that we are more than our bodies? How can we display that the image of God lies within us too? When we change our focus, change happens. It is where the female identifies herself and her pointed passions and behaviors that result in a beautiful picture of womanhood.

The message of the world today seeks to exploit women rather than truly empower them. Today's society encourages women to live self-indulgent by any means necessary. This includes living in conflict with men, women, and children who do not support individual pursuits.

What the media is projecting is not the truth. Women are not created to live disjointed from others around them. Nor do women enjoy living apart from others. Women enjoy relationships and seek to make them better. To keep a community connected, the woman must positively relate to others. Women are the glue between all the people in their community. We are the encouragement of men and the nurturers of children. Women are the keepers of society. This is what we have always done as women.

Join Woman Across Time

I realize this idea and others I hold are not as common as they once were. I also understand that I am not the only woman who shares these ideas. We can consider notable women, past and present, and how they impacted the world by serving others. These women contributed significant efforts in keeping society and sacrificing themselves for the good of others.

Our biblical example includes Queen Esther, a woman who used her position to save others. In the Old Testament Book of the Bible bearing her name, we read about how the king was tricked into writing a death decree for all the Israelites, unaware that his wife belonged to this persecuted nation. Esther entered the king's chamber without being summoned – an offense punishable by death – to save her people (Esther 4). At that moment in time, Esther was a gift to the people around her.

Another Old Testament book of the Bible, Judges, speaks of a woman named Deborah. Deborah, a prophetess, served her people as a judge. She would sit under a tree while the people would bring their matters and concerns to her, and she would instruct them on what to do. One day she called for the leader of the army, Barak, and instructed him to war against another nation. Her words were not enough for Barak, and he requested her presence on the battleground. It was Deborah's guidance and presence that gave assurance to the entire Israelite army, helping them defeat the Canaanite army in Judges 4. At that moment, Deborah was a gift to the people around her.

New Testament examples include Lois and Eunice, who helped form and lead community churches in their homes during times when Christians were persecuted. Together those two women intentionally passed down faith in Jesus Christ to the child in the home, Timothy. He later became the companion of Apostle Paul and a great biblical figure among the believers of Jesus Christ (2 Timothy 1:5, 3:15). The day-to-day efforts of a grandmother and mother led to something beyond themselves that helped change the world. In that day-to-day moment, Lois and Eunice were both a gift to the people around them.

Queen Elizabeth I was a woman who led many by going beyond being uncomfortable and dedicated her very life to the service of the people of England for 44 years. Queen Elizabeth, I chose not to marry as she wanted to devote all her attention to her country and serve the British nation.[3] That decision suited and aided her in marking her reign as a profitable time for the nation. For 44 years, Queen Elizabeth I was a gift to the people around her.

Even more recent examples of living for others include former First Lady Michelle Obama, who sacrificed much to serve the people of the United States of America. Savannah James, the wife of LeBron James, is wholeheartedly dedicated to her family. We see her hand and rarely her face. However, as the significant people in her life excel, her efforts as a wife and mother create a space for them to continue to rise. Both Michelle Obama and Savannah James are a gift to the people around them.

There are women around you and me that have been a gift, as well. I recall sitting with my mentor, Margo Parsons, and asking her what made her the proudest. She began to name the moments she developed people in life and in faith. She went on to mention that the daily decisions to nurture others yielded exponential fruit over time. It called for great sacrifice, but the results impacted generations. Elder Margo was a gift to the people around her.

I make a note of all of these women not to indicate that everything they did was perfect. I am sure it was not. But rather to acknowledge how they intentionally impacted the lives of others. The goal is that these women and other women will inspire the next generation to find value in pouring out their lives for the greater good. Contrary to media messages about women, the greater good is always beyond yourself. This is the message I want to convey—the message which embraces both the old and the new perspective of women. The old quest of women to be the keepers of humanity and the new quest for significance is found when you develop something that goes beyond yourself and allows for generational influence.

Deborah, the Judge, and Queen Elizabeth I both had a to-do list. I imagine there were many days Eunice and Lois were tired from working and still having to raise Timothy.

Maybe Savannah James gave up some of her aspirations for her family; perhaps she is doing exactly what she wants to do. The idea is that the narrative of the woman does not matter; women give of themselves wherever they are.

You give of yourself right where *you* are! You might be exhausted, and at times, uncertain. You might be overextended and overlooked, but you are also still here. So, stick with me, and together, we can join a list of women throughout history who have continued in purpose and thereby impacted their communities and the world.

Womanhood is the intentional, consistent effort to leave your fingerprints on everything you touch in an attempt to help others around you. When you use your time and talent to assist others, you are walking in your design, revealing the real you. You may not feel like it right now, but I assure you that, **you are a gift!**

Reflecting on What You Believe

Take a few moments to pause and reflect on what you've read and your thoughts about womanhood. Record what God reveals about your heart and the truth He shares with you:

1. Why have you decided to read and interact with this book?

2. Do you have a question you hope is answered before the end of the book? If so, write it out here:

    How will you know when this question is answered?

3. What media messages did you hear about womanhood as a child?

4. How has the media positively or negatively influenced your life as a woman?

5. What do you think about the media messages of today concerning women?

6. In what ways have these messages impacted your family life?

Your professional life?

Your romantic life?

7. Identify three media messages about women and write them below:

8. Now identify three biblical messages about women.

9. How are the media messages and biblical messages the same?

   How are they different?

10. Name a famous woman you believe exemplifies womanhood and indicate why you chose her.

A Prayer to Transform Your Mind

Take some time to pray and ask God to reveal to you the impact of today's culture on your view of womanhood. Ask Him to help you release what others think and prepare your heart for what He has said about you. Let's pray together:

Father, thank You that I can bring my heart and mind to You. You already know my struggles with living this life. Many of my struggles come from what others have said and what I think about myself. I have many different voices telling me what I am and what I am not. Today, I ask You to help me not conform to what mainstream says I am but rather transform me by renewing my mind, so I can know the right and acceptable way to live as a woman (Roman 12:1). In Jesus' Name. Amen.

"*The Virtuous Woman did not do everything at once. She did them in seasons. Know your season and you will produce the right fruit.*"

Margo Parsons

Wife, Mother, Community Leader

2

How Did She Do It?

Have you ever noticed a woman who appeared well put together? Maybe she was always happy. Or maybe she never had a bad hair day. Perhaps her life and her car were well organized. Everyone liked her and she seemed to have a near-perfect life. When you leave her presence, you tend to take inventory of your own life, don't you? I think we have all encountered this woman we thought was doing everything well.

I have met this woman on several occasions in my private practice. She comes into my office and tells me just how unhappy she is and how underneath this perfection is a timid and uncertain little girl. She talks about how much she wishes she could just "not care as much." As much as women watch and want *her* life, she watches and wants *your* life.

There is freedom in realizing and owning the fact you were created as a gift right where you are. If you are wearing Prada or pajama pants, the people around you need you and love you. I want to show you the impact you can have when you are convinced that you are a gift to humanity. Being convinced is what we all seek to learn and attain as women. Let's observe this portrait of a woman in Proverbs 31:10-31 (KJV), also identified as the Virtuous Woman. To set this up, King Solomon, the King of Israel and author of Proverbs, is known for the number of women he kept in his kingdom. The last chapter in the book reveals King Solomon's mother is sharing with him the type of woman he ought to marry. This is a mother telling her son about how to identify a godly woman. Today, we read this as a guide to becoming a godly woman.

[10]Who can find a virtuous woman? for her price is far above rubies. [11]The heart of her husband doth safely trust in her, so that he shall have no need of spoil. [12]She will do him good and not evil all the days of her life.

[13]She seeketh wool, and flax, and worketh willingly with her hands. [14]She is like the merchants' ships; she bringeth her food from afar. [15]She riseth also while it is yet night, and giveth meat to her household, and a portion to her maidens.

[16]She considereth a field, and buyeth it: with the fruit of her hands she planteth a vineyard. [17]She girdeth her loins with strength, and strengtheneth her arms. [18]She perceiveth that her merchandise is good: her candle goeth not out by night.

[19]She layeth her hands to the spindle, and her hands hold the distaff. [20]She stretcheth out her hand to the poor; yea, she reacheth forth her hands to the needy.

[21]She is not afraid of the snow for her household: for all her household are clothed with scarlet. [22]She maketh herself coverings of tapestry; her clothing is silk and purple. [23]Her husband is known in the gates, when he sitteth among the elders of the land. [24]She maketh fine linen, and selleth it; and delivereth girdles unto the merchant. [25]Strength and honour are her clothing; and she shall rejoice in time to come.

[26]She openeth her mouth with wisdom; and in her tongue is the law of kindness. [27]She looketh well to the ways of her household, and eateth not the bread of idleness. [28]Her children arise up, and call her blessed; her husband also, and he praiseth her.

[29]Many daughters have done virtuously, but thou excellest them all. [30]Favour is deceitful, and beauty is vain: but a woman that feareth the LORD, she shall be praised. [31]Give her of the fruit of her hands and let her own works praise her in the gates.

Notice how the introductory verse of Proverbs 31:10 declares the value of a woman. It states that a woman walking in the truth or purest form of womanhood is priceless. Proverbs 31:10-31 identifies all the different things this ideal woman did for her family and community. Although there exist many cultural differences between then and now, there are still timeless truths that represent the life of a woman today. The portrait of the virtuous woman provides some key things we all can strive for to help with the God-intended expression of womanhood. So how can we take this cultural passage and apply it today?

If you are like me, then you may have read this passage and thought, *Who can do that?* or *How do you do that?* She seems to have it all together. What I learned is that the passage reflects the *entirety* of a woman's life not a regular *day* in her life. The things she was able to accomplish she did through consistency, not through compounding. There were different times in her life when she was selling things at the market. And other times when she was caring for the needy. She consistently did what she committed to do. She did not do all these things at the same time throughout her life. Instead, she did what was necessary and reasonable at the moment. And when that moment passed, she did something else.

We tend to feel intimidated by the image of the woman described in Proverbs 31 and immediately feel as though we fall short. That is not the intent of the passage. This woman's description is to invite and encourage women to be virtuous. It is also to help us relate to this ideal woman and all other women. To be true and pure is not as far-off as we may think.

I have taken the liberty of imagining the virtuous woman's inner dialogue. Remember, the Virtuous Woman is a portrait of a woman. She is you and me. Imagine with me what a daily diary entry may have looked like for her today.

January 12th

I am so tired, but I want to write about my day. It was a good day. Everything did not go as planned, but I was able just to keep going, and it turned out well. I started today well since there was milk in the fridge for my teens. They love cereal, and I have to keep it stocked. Sometimes I miss it, but today there was milk for the children's cereal and milk for my coffee, too. So, everybody won. After dropping off the children at school, I was able to sit and look at the bank account and what was available for our upcoming vacation. Here is where I got disappointed. I was hoping the sale of my garments would mean more money in the house, but it brought just enough to help cover the bills. I have some more garments left, so hopefully, I can get the last few sold before the end of the month.

My husband asked me to take over the finances back in October. And while I like knowing just how much money we have, it does stress me out to know exactly where we are and what is needed. He says he trusts me to do it and knows that I will manage the money well. So, I do it. He says not managing the money helps him focus on making more money. And I have seen this to be true. The income has increased over the past three months.

I committed to helping organize the women's closet at the domestic violence shelter. When I got there, the women were lined up seeking clothing for their children and themselves. It made me sad and grateful at the same time. As I pulled out my bag of clothes to donate, one of the women ran over. She said, "I already like what you are wearing. I know you have some good stuff." We went through the bag together, and she was able to fit a few of the items from my closet. She was so happy and said she felt beautiful in new clothes. Thank You, Lord, for allowing me to give and see the impact of my giving. I am so glad I pushed through and kept my commitment today.

After serving there, I called my husband, and he told me he got a promotion today. His boss was impressed with his work and thought his idea for the company last month was great. The company made a considerable profit, and the boss decided to promote my husband. I was excited, listening to him talk. I wanted to but chose not to remind him that the idea his boss loved was my idea. Either way, we win. With this promotion, we may be able to take the vacation I wanted.

I did work today, and while at lunch with my friend, she shared with me that she was having trouble dealing with her mother. Her mother is aging, and she has many decisions to make about her care. The more she talked, I could hear her fear and stress of making the right decision for her mother and her family. I listened before speaking and prayed to myself that God would give me the words to encourage her. Hopefully, I planted some seeds today and she will not feel alone during this time. She has been there for me when I was having difficulties with my oldest. I want to do the same and help my friend carry this burden during this time. Together we researched her options before returning to work.

As I was coming home, I heard that it might snow tonight. I knew that we had some groceries but not enough if we were trapped for two days. I had to rush to the store, pick up the kids, cook dinner, check homework, make sure everyone bathed, had a daily reflection with the kids, prayed, and finish up some last-minute work documents. I am not sure how it all worked out, but I got it done in three hours. I am exhausted but think I can sleep well knowing we have what we need if I wake up to snow tomorrow.

Just as I was prepared to go to bed, one of the ladies from the women's shelter called to share that her time there expired, and she needs housing by tomorrow. I am not quite sure how that is going to work since tomorrow is Saturday and places are closed. What makes it even more difficult is that she is still in hiding. So, I must keep her anonymous while still finding a place for her to go. I want to help her, but I am not quite sure how to right now. I hope that I can think more clearly after sleeping tonight.

As always, I will end this journal with how I saw God today. Today, I saw God: 1) as the One who provided my husband with favor and more provision for our family; 2) in the faces of the women at the women's shelter; 3) as the One who ordered my steps until I finished my daily tasks for my family.

Thank You, Lord. And I love You!

One more thing...Tonight, my husband told me that he is still struggling with that secret sin. This hurt to hear, but I am glad I know. I pray for him continuously. He knows God loves him and shared that he feels so guilty receiving the blessing of a promotion from the Lord while struggling with this sin. I told him that I love him and that together we can continue to pray and work on turning away from this sin. I thanked him for telling me because we promised we would tell each other when either of us is struggling with sin. Ugh...Lord, help us move through this.

I wrote this fictional journal entry considering the Scripture references about the Virtuous Woman. However, Scripture gives us a portrait of this ideal woman and it tells us only how she *responded* to life. We know what she did. We are not privy to what she encountered or what she thought. I believe that it does not matter because she experienced everything you and I experience. She was around men, women, and children. There is no doubt that she experienced pain, joy, disappointment, and anger, just like you and me. I do not believe her life was perfect. I also do not believe she was perfect, but I do believe her response to life was purposeful.

To further this point, take a few moments to highlight the parts of her day that correspond to the Scripture verses we read in Proverbs 31:10-31.

Breaking it Down

Although the Virtuous Woman is married, her life example is applicable for both married and single women. This passage is intended to help identify God's intention for women. Again, her circumstances may not match our lives exactly, yet there is so much we can learn from her. There are many noble things she has done. Our goal is not to *do* the exact things she has done. The goal is to approach our life and circumstances the way she approached life. Considering this, show yourself grace along the way to becoming "a woman to be praised."

To make the image of the Virtuous Woman attainable, I have categorized her traits into four categories. The Proverbs 31 Woman was trustworthy, productive, well-kept, and wise.

Let's look at this more closely.

Trustworthy

In relationship to her husband and other people, the Proverbs 31 Woman was trustworthy. Proverbs 31:11-12, 20, and 23 states that her husband had full confidence in her and lacked nothing of value. He knew her heart toward him was that she wanted to see him prosper and never lack anything. This must have been communicated through both her actions and deeds. He knew that she was the same toward him in every situation. Trust refers to how you can predict a person will behave. If this is true, the woman's speech and behavior were predictable toward everyone in her life and especially her husband. She was the same, regardless of what may have changed during her life. He had a mental picture of her that made him feel safe.

Others, also, had a mental picture of the Virtuous Woman that made them feel safe. She attended to the poor, and they accepted her ministry to them. They felt safe with her. As we relate to all the people in our lives, our goal is to have consistent speech and behavior where others are confident that they know us, and they feel safe with us. Being trustworthy is necessary to foster relationships. As women, we relate best with others when we are trustworthy.

Productive

The Proverbs 31 Woman was productive. She was always doing something with her hands. We see this clearly in Proverbs 31:13-19, 21, 27-28, and 31. She was productive as she continuously developed and maintained her household. This included household chores and earning money. She took on the needs of the home and proudly cared for her family. She also demonstrated there is so much more to the biblical view of womanhood than domestic support.

Taking care of people around you, at times, includes leaving home and finding a place in the market. We understand that she was a seamstress and sold her garments. She provided belts for the other salesmen in the market (verse 24). We also know that she had other streams of income in that she bought and planted a vineyard –another transaction says in the market – (verse 16). Proverbs 31:31 suggests this as it states, "Honor her for all her hands have done, let her works bring her praise at the city gate." The City Gate was a public place. Sometimes people are recognized publicly for the things done privately. More often, people are recognized publicly for the things done publicly. We are encouraged to honor this woman for what she did both privately and publicly. She was not confined to her house alone as a gift to just her family, she was productive in and out of the house.

> *She was doing exactly what she was gifted to do and that was enough.*

So many women struggle with the idea of working at home or away from home. The truth is that there is no right or wrong way. As a woman, you are designed to produce. Whether you work in the home or work outside the home, you can contribute. The Virtuous Woman was not idle, nor was she aimlessly busy. It seems she was doing exactly what she was gifted to do and understood that was enough.

Well-kept

The Virtuous Woman was also well-kept. Throughout this proverb, we see her consistently engaged with clothing.

This could have been cultural, but Proverbs 31:22 is about how she dresses. Unlike the clothing she dresses others with, her clothing is described as linen material, having the color of purple. Just like today, the material of her clothing determines the value of the garment. The color added another luxury element since purple required a mixture of dyes. The idea is that she was well-dressed. A well-dressed woman is one who considers her appearance. Many of the verses indicate that she was making clothes. The writer emphasized how she dressed herself to reveal how she considered her own appearance, too. She was not overly obsessed with how she looked. However, it was important for her not to appear less than her value. The passage is not so much about what she wore, as many Scriptures discuss what she did while wearing these fine garments. However, it makes mention of her clothes to tell us something else about her. When you are well-kept, you communicate to others that you desire the best for yourself.

Beauty is desirable. Yet, there is more to womanhood than how you look, and even men know this. We should not base being a gift solely on what we look like or what we are wearing. In defining a woman, appearance can never stand alone. Attention from others based only on your physical traits makes you an object to be used rather than a gift to be valued.

Using your dress to highlight your physical characteristics is sure to result in the abuse of the gift that you are. When you only focus—and allow others to solely focus—on your bodily appearance, your talents and abilities to rule and have dominion are diminished. A woman can eliminate the mystery of her value by immediately revealing her value in how she keeps herself.

Wise

A woman relates to others in wisdom. Proverbs 31:26 indicates that the Virtuous Woman was wise in her speech: "She opens her mouth with wisdom; and the law of kindness is on her *tongue." Chokmah* is the Hebrew word here, which means "be wise in mind or word, to show thyself wise or teach wisdom."[1] Proverbs 2:6 reminds us that the Lord gives wisdom; out of his mouth comes knowledge and understanding. To say the Virtuous Woman was wise is to say she knew the right thing to say and/or do when with others. This wisdom came from the time she devoted to God. The Virtuous Woman spent time with the Lord to gain personal wisdom, as well as wisdom with which to instruct others.

We cannot have the exact life of the Proverbs 31 Woman; however, we can obtain wisdom and love from the same place she did. Seeking God will enable us to gain a greater understanding and walk in love. The more time we spend with God and receive from Him, the more we can give this same gift to others. When God gently corrects us, we will know how to correct others gently. When we know the mercy and kindness of God, we can extend mercy and kindness toward others. When we do so, everyone "will see our good works and glorify our Father which is in heaven" (Matthew 5:16).

What we are learning is that biblical womanhood is exemplified in how we speak to our husbands and others. The words a woman utters reflect her true beauty. To consider God before speaking and to be guided by the law of love creates for a beautiful person and a woman whom any person would want to be around. On the contrary, the woman who lacks discretion or wisdom in her speech and deeds is described as a "gold ring in a swine's snout" (Proverbs 11:22). This woman is also a gift, but people are hesitant to receive it because of what they will endure to obtain it. A woman's gift is appreciated when she uses wisdom and kindness toward others.

A woman relates to others with wisdom.

Your family members, coworkers, and people in your social circles, all anticipate you dealing lovingly toward them. We know this is not always easy, but it is a gift we give to them. Living in righteousness will bring the fruit of righteousness in your life. Living in integrity, wisdom, and self-control comes with peace of mind and a good reputation.

Remember, the Proverbs 31 woman was not perfect. This was an ode to all that she did right. She shows us the gift we are and how to relate to man and mankind as a gift. Knowing that she was human, we can have the confidence that what she possessed we too can obtain. The traits she exemplified are things we can all develop if we choose.

Possessing these traits will add to the gifts we can offer others. When we are not trustworthy, productive, well-kept, and wise, we can create a distraction or delay in others receiving the gift that we are.

The Virtuous Woman took care of everyone. She cared for her husband, children, and the community. That was her focus. What is not revealed is how she cared for herself. We cannot point to a verse that proves she rested, but we can prove it by the compilation of all the verses.

Taking Time to Rest

The Proverbs 31 passage discusses how the woman woke when it was dark and how her lamp did not go out at night. Certainly, the idea is not suggesting sleep deprivation. I think this makes the point that she was productive at all costs. It is not possible to achieve what she continuously displayed while sleep deprived. I do not know if you have missed some hours in your night, but sleep deprivation impacts your productivity and your relationships. Your brain is slowed, and you become unpleasant to be around. Continuously neglecting herself would have hindered her ability to care for others. Rather the idea is that she was focused and busy producing in life. She was not producing for herself or on her own. She worked alongside God to produce what He wanted in the ways He wanted. And that is wise.

Her display of wisdom is seen in what she did but also refers to ethical and religious living. In following God, she must have been aware and compliant with the command to honor the Sabbath, which is the command to rest by ceasing from labor (Exodus 20:8-10). God created us, male and female, to refresh and reflect, which increases our ability to do His will.

We must honor the Lord with our gifts but also with our obedience to rest. Making time to stop work and honor the Lord is not only for our spiritual health but also for our emotional and mental health. It is through a relationship with God that we can successfully care for self and others.

We must honor God with our gifts but also with our obedience to rest.

Self-care is anything that is scheduled or spontaneous that allows you to ask the question, *What do I need right now?* It includes times of relaxation but also reflection. Pausing and reflecting about where we are in our circles of influence can aid in matching the intent with the behaviors. Making sure the people in our lives hear our messages requires that we identify the message and prepare to deliver it. That requires reflection and relaxation – self-care.

Many women struggle with taking care of themselves. The demands placed on your life and mine appear to leave us little to no room for ourselves. This is an illusion. If God commanded us to rest, rest must be available. Simply knowing you have permission to rest can help you enjoy your womanhood. There is space available for you to rest. Yet, you must carve out space.

The Sabbath (which means "rest") was dedicated.[2] It was set apart from the other days of the week. For the Virtuous Woman, resting was a part of her routine. For many women today, rest is subjective, and as a result, the cares of others override personal care. It is not until we are exhausted, frustrated, and easily disturbed that we consider taking a break. When we value our gift, we will preserve ourselves so that we can continue to give the gift of ourselves.

The Virtuous Woman completed so many noble things throughout her life. This picture of womanhood she provides is an encouragement that there is grace to which we can carry out the tasks God has assigned every woman. He knows what you can do and what things are a struggle for you. He does not expect all of us to be alike. He does, however, expect us to reflect His image of trustworthiness, productivity, being well-kept, and exercising wisdom. He also expects us to find rest while being a gift to others.

There are many ways to refresh yourself as a woman. Of course, our different personalities and preferences will curb this decision. The very first step of self-care includes being honest with yourself. You are taking care of yourself when you are honest about where you are and what you need. Once you allow yourself to desire a break, you are more inclined to carve out space for yourself to get that break.

---

*The first step to self-care is being
honest with yourself.*

Trying to Do it All

I remember feeling completely exhausted. Trying to care for my husband, children, clients, and my community was taxing. It was not that I was doing the wrong things. I was doing the things God gifted me to do. I was just not taking the time to rest, which is what I desperately needed. I needed to restructure my life but seemingly could not find the time to do it. The result was that I was not myself. I no longer wanted to be a woman. I did not desire to be a man, but I thought being a woman was an unfortunate place in life. Looking back, that was a disturbing thought when all I needed was to take time to rest. A guilt-free nap allowed me to refresh myself. I recommend before even taking a break, that you allow yourself to believe you need one. This is how you enjoy whatever you choose to refresh yourself.

Many times we lie to ourselves by believing things have to be done immediately. We continue in that and may even tell ourselves "If I don't do it no one else will." When we place these demands on ourselves it leaves little room for rest. Then we find ourselves upset and angry with the people we seek to care for. We can release ourselves and improve our relationships all at the same time. We do this by giving ourselves grace and pacing ourselves.

When God gives us grace He extends his favor toward us even when we are undeserving. He is kind toward us when we deserve something else. If God, knowing everything He does about us can give us grace, we ought to give ourselves grace. We do this by allowing ourselves to leave some things undone. You and I cannot do everything today, this week, or maybe even this month. We do what we can and trust God will allow us to complete the eternal works before leaving this earth. If you are not sure what is the eternal work, let me tell you that it is not folding laundry or deboning chicken. The eternal works are the things that last beyond us. Those are the tasks we make sure we do. And in everything else we give ourselves grace.

Charles Hummel wrote a book called *Tyranny of the Urgent*[3] I recommend reading this book to further aid in knowing the difference between what is urgent and what is important in life. When we focus on the urgent we often feel exhausted and unaccomplished. However, the important things in life are less demanding but yield a greater reward. I suggest identifying what is important to you and filtering everything in life through this lens. By doing so you can focus on caring for those you love while still taking care of yourself. You can walk in truth, purity, and the beauty of being a woman.

"Gimme A Break"

The idea of self-care may sound selfish to some. I want to clarify that it is not the idea of seeking personal gain without thought of others. Self-care is about balancing work and rest so that you minimize and/or manage stress and stress-related issues. Self-care is a preventative measure to remain selfless. Ultimately, when we are well physically, emotionally, and spiritually, we have something to give others.

When you are taking care of yourself in a healthy way, you are indirectly taking care of those around you. When we are not our best, our interaction with others is not the best. A lack of sleep, poor eating, and little reflection can impact the best intentions to perform or relate well to others. Don't let your efforts to help be lost to your ability to relate.

I have included a list of self-care activities that you may want to consider as you carve out space for yourself. I hope the list aids you in developing and maintaining this special time for yourself. This is the moment where you recharge by connecting with your Creator, God, and allowing Him to reveal your heart. The things on the list are small enough to implement without changing your lifestyle but big enough to create change in the way you approach your life. If you already have a stable self-care regimen, I encourage you to stick with it.

Please check each activity you do weekly.

Exercise	
Eat regular, healthy meals	
Get enough sleep	
Attend preventative health appointments	
Take time off from work and house obligations	
Talk about my problems	
Read a book	
Learn something new	
Have stimulating conversations	
Regular physical intimacy with a spouse	
Spend time with people I enjoy	
Laugh	
Pray	
Behave consistently with moral and faith values	
Meet new people	
Say "no" to new excessive activities	
Keep in touch with old friends	
Keep a journal	
Talk to my spouse	
Ask for help	
Go on vacations or staycations	
Cater family meals	
Go to the park	
Hire a housekeeper	
Go to the salon	
Attend faith services	
Go for a bike ride	
Listen to my favorite music	
Create a gratitude list	
Turn my phone off for a day	
Practice deep breathing	
Attend a support group	

"In all you do, don't lose yourself."

Vernetha White

A Friend

Reflecting on Your Expression of Womanhood

Take a few moments to pause and reflect as a means of sorting through what you've read and your own thoughts about womanhood. Record what God reveals about your heart and the truth He shares with you:

1. In what ways are you different from the Virtuous Woman?

2. In what ways are you similar to her?

3. Using the scale below, rate yourself on your display of the four character traits of the Virtuous Woman outlined in this chapter:

    1=not at all   5=sometimes   10=always

    Trustworthy_____Well-Kept_____
    Productive_____Wise_____

4. Is there any area you want to improve?

If so, what is your plan to develop the trait(s)?

5. The Virtuous Woman was intentional about taking care of her home. Read Proverbs 14:1. List the ways you care for your home.

Are there any ways you tear it down?

6. Do you have a designated time for self-care? Why or Why not?

7. How do you know when it is time to care for yourself?

"Then the rib which the Lord God had taken from man, He made into a woman, and He brought her to the man."

Genesis 2:22 (KJV)

3

Created to Care

Maybe you're still not convinced you are a gift. You may be saying to yourself: *If I am a gift, why do I not feel like one?* As you continue to read, I will explain how I concluded that I am a gift. I trust you will come to the same conclusion. Understanding your purpose and design gives you greater confidence, self-worth, and value. If you are clear on your purpose and design, you are more apt to fulfill your purpose and find satisfaction.

I hope that you, too, will explore this view and share it with other women. We all experience life differently. I am convinced that every experience is an opportunity to draw us closer to the truth of why we are here and a tool to help us understand the truth.

Where can I find the truth? There are so many sources claiming to be an authority on womanhood. It is important to identify your starting point and identify what you are holding as true. This may provide a clear picture of why and how you have been living out your expression of womanhood. My faith was the starting point in finding my answer. You will be challenged and comforted by the truth found in God's Holy Word.

The Bible is an authoritative source. Although written by men, the Bible was inspired by God. The ageless truths give credence to the written Word of God. The Bible is a historical book, but also a prophetic book. The Bible has been proven to tell about both the past and the future (2 Peter 1:20-21). The Word of God is eternal. We can live according to its truth (1 Timothy 3:16-17).

The truth of the Word of God is the basis for this book, and the truth I am learning to live as outlined in Genesis 2:22. This chapter of the Bible emphasizes the creation of woman. Genesis 2 reveals the woman was created out of the man, presented to the man, and then finally presented to the rest of creation with the same purpose of dominating nature. It would appear the creation narrative yields an excellent starting point as it immediately highlights the woman's intended purpose: the woman is God's gift to man to help subdue the earth. Read Genesis 2:15-25 slowly to gain an understanding of the creation account of the woman. I have provided it below for your convenience. You will understand so much more of the context of what I am writing if you first read it for yourself.

> [15] Then the Lord God took [the man and put him in the garden of Eden to tend and keep it. [16] And the Lord God commanded the man, saying, "Of every tree of the garden you may freely eat; [17] but of the tree of the knowledge of good and evil you shall not eat, for in the day that you eat of it you shall surely die."

[18] And the Lord God said, "It is not good that man should be alone; I will make him a helper comparable to him." [19] Out of the ground the Lord God formed every beast of the field and every bird of the air, and brought them to Adam to see what he would call them. And whatever Adam called each living creature, that was its name. [20] So Adam gave names to all cattle, to the birds of the air, and to every beast of the field. But for Adam there was not found a helper comparable to him.

[21] And the Lord God caused a deep sleep to fall on Adam, and he slept; and He took one of his ribs, and closed up the flesh in its place. [22] Then the rib which the Lord God had taken from man He made into a woman, and He brought her to the man. [23] And Adam said: "This is now bone of my bones And flesh of my flesh; She shall be called Woman, Because she was taken out of Man."

[24] Therefore a man shall leave his father and mother and be joined to his wife, and they shall become one flesh. [25] And they were both naked, the man and his wife, and were not ashamed.

How You Were Designed

The solution to living life well as a woman is to understand your purpose and design. Genesis 2 tells us God made the woman and "presented" her to the man. God spent days creating, and He shared His creation with the man (Genesis 2:15).

God then turned His thoughts toward the man and identified a need in him. God's thoughts are what led to the belief that the woman was a gift given to the man.

Genesis 2:18 shares this thought of God: "It is not good for man to be alone." The word *alone* means singularly[1]. God was present with the man but still considered him singular or solitary. He wanted to give the man something that would benefit him just as the other creatures with a similar likeness were coupled. The man was the only creation without an equal. So, God created a woman so that the man would not be alone.

The creation of woman, the Scriptures states, was on the sixth day after God formed man from the dust. Then He formed the woman by removing a part of the man while he slept (Gen 1:27; 2:22). God made the woman because He knew what was best for the man. He gave him a creature similar in nature yet different in function. Matthew Henry's Commentary on Genesis 2:22 explains the creation of woman so poetically and also provides both biological facts and societal functions:

> "That the woman was made of a rib out of the side of Adam; not made out of his head to rule over him, nor out of his feet to be trampled upon by him, but out of his side to be equal with him, under his arm to be protected, and near his heart to be beloved."[2]

Maybe you were taught and believe that the woman is secondary to the man. It is tough to find fulfillment in second place. By creative accounts, God created the woman second, and throughout human history, she is treated as second, but she is not secondary. The Bible confirms the dual dominion in Genesis 1:27-28 when it says, "So God created mankind in His own image; in the image of God He created them; male and female He created them; God blessed them and said to them, 'Be fruitful and increase in number; fill the earth and subdue it.'" I am so grateful that God's Word clarifies this misjudgment of our value; it affirms the value of women and asserts that women subdue the earth alongside the man.

Woman, as defined in Genesis 2:22, is from the Hebrew word *ISHSHAH* meaning woman, wife, and female. It is the feminine form of the word *IYSH*, meaning man, mankind, individual, champion, and servant.[3] If being a man means "individual, champion, and servant," what is the feminine meaning of the word? If man and woman are alike, yet distinct, it must mean one individual, champion, and servant is a man and the other individual, champion, and servant is a woman. The immediate difference between the man and woman in Genesis 2 is that she was created to fulfill a need.

Immediately we see the woman as *filling the gap* and *meeting a need*. Her existence was *needed*—the way she was crafted suited what the man needed. Before saying or doing anything, she was a *gift*. The Great "I AM" created a woman as a gift.

The Word of God tells us that the woman was *presented* to the man. This means that God *gave* the woman to the man, much like a gift is given from one person to another. Scripture goes on to say that man was pleased to have received her. He immediately recognized that he could relate to her and declared, *"This is bone of my bone and flesh of my flesh..."* (Genesis 2:23*).*

In these few verses, we can see the purpose and design of womanhood. The creator, God, purposefully created the woman to be a companion for the man. The woman was no doubt made *for* the man. Here lies the desire each gender has for one another. As the recipient, man is yearning to relate and connect to the gift. As a gift, the woman is constructed to relate and connect to the man. As the man and woman looked at one another, they intuitively knew they were alike in image and they fit. How can one look at himself and not want to care for his image? This goes for both the man and the woman. While they are mostly similar, they are different in function hence the need for one another.

The function of the woman is to help and so God granted the man a helper: "I will make a *helper* comparable to him" (Genesis 2:18). This word helper or *azer*, means aid or helper.[4] Thus, God intended to make valuable help to the man in the form of a female champion, a woman. Women are a necessary gift to all. Without the male-female dynamic, things were undone in the garden. God continued creating until He rested. He did not rest until after the woman was presented to the man (Gen 1:27).

The woman is a treasured helper.

I understand that this is tough to accept or acknowledge. If we believe in the creation story, then we must believe God used wisdom during all of His creative activities. In wisdom, God created His best. If we believe this, then we must believe this about all the things He created. If we agree that God created the woman, as the Word outlines, the conclusion is that the woman was created for the man.

When God first gave the woman to the man, she was to be his companion or partner. The Lord emphasized this design and purpose in other verses that show the relationship between the male and female.. These verses include "He who finds a wife finds a good thing," (Proverbs 18:22), and "a prudent wife is from the Lord" (Proverbs 19:14).

The woman was given to the man as a *helpmate*. Adam looked at this gift and immediately stated, "This is now bone of my bone and flesh of my flesh" (Genesis 2:23). He not only identified with the woman but *received* her. His reception and embrace indicate that he received the gift, the treasured help.

We can fight against this idea and struggle through life, or we can accept it and learn to live in a relationship with a man where both men and women are satisfied. When the man accepted the gift, and the woman behaved as the gift, something great happened. Accepting the truth that a wise God created man and woman requires accepting that He also made them interdependent. God created the woman as a treasured helper to the man and to mankind.

Contributions of Women

History is filled with the efforts of women and men. The things we build, create, and destroy are written on walls, scrolls, sacred texts, and books. The history of people shows us striving to have dominion and to subdue the earth. Sometimes there are considerable distinctions between the characters of the story in clarifying whether they were male or female. However, each gender has its greatness recorded in the centuries of the earth. What is true about every century, every culture, every class, and every faith of people is that women have had their hand in earth's tapestry. Her efforts at times may be hidden or quieted, but without her presence, the earth could not remain. This includes childbirth and child-rearing but is not exclusive to the life-giving qualities of women.

As the Divine Creator, God nurtures His creation. He is committed to the care of the earth and its inhabitants. His supernatural power in creating the systems of the earth sustains us today. As God cares for humanity in providing life-sustaining and life-developing needs, women care for our communities. Women have a way of developing people, things, and ideas. This is what we do, both intentionally and unintentionally. As a result, the role of a woman continues through centuries, cultures, race, class, and faith. She is consistently planning and producing something. I would dare say that a woman inspired everything created by man. She nurtures the soul and ideas of future generations. Nurturing becomes a way to walk alongside man in the dominion of the earth. She is necessary because she is a gift.

As women, we all breathe life into something. Typically, it is other people: a husband, a child, a sister, a coworker, a niece, a nephew, a neighbor, and so on. Sometimes it is not breathing life into people directly, but into situations that will benefit others. While the differences between men and women are many, I believe the most considerable difference is the gift within women to nurture. To nurture is to give care and concern to people and things in such a way that development and growth are present. The gift of the woman is the critical care required to foster transformation within people, places, and things. She encourages those around her, either in word or deed. Her gift is so great that even in solitude, the woman seeks something to care for and look after. The design is so precise that when she no longer cares or nurtures, she experiences a physical, emotional, mental, and spiritual decline. Nurturing is the gift of God *within* the woman.

From generation to generation, we see the woman being a gift to others in her circle. This is her purpose and design. Failing to embrace this would create great turmoil and struggle within the woman and lead to great detriment to yourself and others. Embracing this truth allows the people around you who receive that care to identify you as a gift given to them—a gift they need and can enjoy. Whether or not people tell you, they can benefit considerably from what God has placed within you, making you a gift tailor-made for them.

Finding Fulfillment

The expression of your gift will bring you fulfillment. You will find joy in giving your gift of nurturing and care to others.

It may not always be easy, and there may be moments you may want to quit. But when you are actively *gifting* it is a joy.

I am reminded of a young lady who came into my office. She was single and focused on her career. While she loved what she was doing, she honestly struggled at times with giving her best to her patients. This young lady was certain of what God called her to do. The people around her celebrated her work and confirmed her. Yet, how she saw herself often delayed her responses in doing what she loves to do. She viewed herself as too sensitive, inadequate, anxious, and taken for granted. She hated being so agreeable and doing for everyone else but herself.

Her agreeable personality frequently led her to say "yes" to things she did not want to do, believing this helped her maintain relationships. She soon realized that she was frequently asked to do more and expected by others to do more. She felt taken advantage of and was convinced there was no reciprocity.

During her time of working with me, we addressed her self-image, assertive communication, and managing anxiety. We confirmed that God loves her and created her for good works. Her skills and abilities were valuable and something she did enjoy using. Once convinced of having something to give, she learned how to give it rather than feeling like it was being taken from her.

We discussed giving our gifts by talking to the Gift Giver, God, instead of the receiver. When people asked her to do things, she first learned to consult God to determine if her hand needed to touch a person or a task. This allowed her to willingly give the gift of herself. This also allowed her to value what she realized was not for everyone. The woman noticed when she prayed about the people and things she was to develop or maintain, she was able to give herself as a gift and was received as one.

I told you this woman's story because I think you – and every woman – can relate to her in some way. Maybe you struggle to see your gift as valuable. If we stop and honestly think about who we are and what we are doing, we may discover that we are more significant than we realize. It could be that we know we bring value but seem unsure of whom to share our gifts with, so we give our gifts away to people who take us for granted. I encourage you to return to our Creator, God. Allow Him to show you your value within. Let His Spirit guide you in your efforts here on earth. Let Him show you eternal works so you are not doing exhausting works. In turn, your approach to womanhood and life will allow for increased productivity so that you can be the gift and give the gift to others as God-ordained.

Remember, you are the gift God has given to the people around you. It is not that you are perfect, but you are perfect for your family, your husband, your children, your friends, your coworkers, and your community. When we start to see ourselves as a gift, then the way we interact with others will be free and not forced. It will come from a natural, healthy place as we are confident in who we are and what we are doing.

Just as God uniquely handmade Eve to meet Adam's needs, His hand has made you too. There are so many unique things about you that the world needs; your creativity your leadership, your organizational skills, your listening ear or wise word, and even your servant attitude is needed in the lives of those around you. You and I are indeed the handiwork of God, created in Christ Jesus to do good works, which God prepared in advance for us to do (Ephesian 2:10).

We all have different experiences and situations in which we are "given" so that we can be a gift. You are where you are because you have something to offer your situation. God looked and decided that the people surrounding you, needed you. He gifted them with your presence and personality. Others may, at times, confirm your value, and you may even hear of its impact in your circles of influence. The compliments and encouraging words people give you often speak of the gift you bring. It may sound like, "You are so talented" or "You are so funny." Sometimes it may be something that you have yet to embrace yourself, but others see it in you. They may say things like, "You are a great leader," or "You are a great teacher." Your gift is unique to you and valuable for those, it is intended to help.

Be Intentional

Let me be clear here: your value is not determined by others! You are already valuable, and you only express it to others when you walk in principle and intention of being a gift. The response of people does *not validate* your gift. It may *confirm* what you already know is true. At times we may struggle to believe that we are a gift. We may look at our abilities and determine that we are not enough. We may compare ourselves to others and say that we are lacking.

There may even be times when people devalue us. This does not discount that we were created to be a gift. We were created to be a blessing to others. We are given, presented, and brought to the people in our lives. Sometimes they immediately recognize our value. Other times, it takes a while for the discovery of who we are to come to light.

So, what does "I am a gift" truly mean? *I am a gift* means that I am given to help others and that within me is the ability to nurture the change necessary in my circles of *life*. It is the belief that the image of God within you is valuable, and that you are free to express that in every space you enter, with everything your hands may touch. As a woman, you were created *to fill a gap* and or *fulfill a need*. This declaration is not made in arrogance. Instead, it is the battle cry of every woman to reclaim her intent and purpose when challenged to live for herself. It is a reminder you are most satisfied relating to others and bringing change to the lives of men, women, and children around you.

"I am a gift" is what you say to encourage yourself to do those things that honor God. When you feel as though you are growing weak in your resolve to *fill the gap* or *help others*, declare "I am a gift." It is what you remind yourself when you are neglecting self-care, which is necessary to continue living for Christ.

You were created to care and nurture, and that has so many different forms for so many different women. Embracing this truth can help you in the moments when you have a great struggle in carrying out your purpose. A gift is valuable. A gift is given. I will say it again: *You are a gift.*

Reflecting on the Truth About Womanhood

Take a few moments to pause and reflect on what you've read about womanhood. Record what God reveals about your heart and the truth He shares with you:

1. What is your authoritative source for understanding womanhood?

2. God created woman as a treasured "help." What is your initial response to hearing this truth?

    In what ways do you think women *help*?

3. What Scripture can you use to remind yourself of your value in how you were created?

4. What do you identify as the value you bring to your circles of influence?

5. How have others in your community confirmed this gift?

6. What was your reaction to the idea of being "given" to your circles and what ideology of yours does this challenge?

7. Do you think there is a difference between being useful and being used? If so, how can you tell the difference?

8. Take a moment to compare your beliefs about womanhood with your experiences in womanhood. Do your beliefs match your expression of womanhood? How?

A Prayer for Truth and Freedom

We outlined the thoughts and intentions of God when He created you as a woman. This may have been news to you or it could have reiterated what you already believe in your heart. Take some time to talk with God about what it means to be a "treasured help." Ask Him to help you receive this truth in both your head and your heart.

> *Father, I know that Your Word is true and that it stands for all time. I can see throughout history that women have continued to be a gift to men, other women, and children. Lord, I want to help. I want to care, and I also want to be cared for. Help me receive this truth that I am a "treasured helper." I trust You to help me be a gift in the lives of other people. May You remove every argument that tells me otherwise. I declare You are wise, and truth lies with You. You promised that I would know and accept in my heart the truth, and it would set me free (John 8:32). Your Word is true (John 17:17). Set me free. In Jesus' Name, Amen.*

"It is not good for man to be alone. I will make a helper suitable for him."

Genesis 2:18

4

You Are a Gift
to Man

For centuries, women have asked the same question: "How do I live with a man?" It seems each generation of women chooses a handful of ways to relate to men. Women have either been behind the man, beside the man, or in front of the man. It is no wonder we remain uncertain of our roles as we still think we are either enslaved to the man or disconnected from him. The rest of us fall in between this continuum, searching for a socially acceptable place to land.

Women before me, the women born in my generation, and the women in generations behind me will all fight the same internal battle. Women have continued to ask how to live with a man because the truth is the two sexes are interdependent. No matter how much we try, we cannot live apart from one another, and so this battle continues. It is a futile battle to live a life separate from a man. We must learn to live life as intended...*alongside* men.

Let us seek to land on the truth that man and women were created to exist interdependently. It is not an archaic idea but both scientific and biblical that women and men relate for the sake of humanity. Both the male and female are needed to push forward the earth. I am speaking of procreation but also beyond child-bearing. The interdependence of men and women is what makes the dominion of the earth possible. Without doubt, 1 Corinthians 11:11-12 communicates this truth:

> "[11]Nevertheless, neither *is* man independent of woman, nor woman independent of man, in the Lord. [12]For as woman *came* from man, even so man also *comes* through woman; but all things are from God."

A Gift is Given

How was Eve a gift to Adam? We discussed how the gift within the woman is to nurture. With this gift alongside him, Adam no longer had to rule and have dominion alone. As a recipient of the woman, the man received a useful helpmate: the woman champion. The woman came alongside him and subdued the earth. The quality of his life improved because of her design. Her presence allowed for the man to develop and thrive differently in the garden. She immediately changed his life. He had a counterpart to work alongside him and help him fulfill God's assignment on his life. Because of Eve, Adam was able to multiply on the earth.

His image would continue for generations and centuries. That was the beautiful union of the man and woman. The interdependence was desired, and humankind was perfect.

The woman immediately changed the man's life in the garden.

God created humanity with dominion and authority to rule over all living things on the earth. He created man first, then the woman, and gave the woman to the man. The man saw the woman as more than his equal; he saw her as himself – his flesh and his blood. The idea that women are subservient to men was not the intention of the Creator. This misinterpretation of the *gift* is the cause of many women feeling undervalued.

As we look at the interaction between men and women today, we see something entirely different than what was present in Genesis 2:22. The man is no longer considered the recipient of the gift, and the woman is no longer considered a gift. Both men and women alike promote the idea that we can live independently of one another. We blame one another for our failures and continue to point the finger just as Adam and Eve did in the garden after the Fall (Genesis 3). This hostile relationship has left us to relate to sexual deviance and not earthly domination. The man and woman, while of the same kind, have become enemies toward one another.

Reclaiming Your Lost Gift

If you have been the victim of domestic violence or op-pression, including sexual abuse, human trafficking, dis-crimination, name-calling, and so on, I understand it can be challenging to read this chapter. Due to your personal experi-ences or having heard similar stories of other women, it may be difficult for you to believe that men would treat you as a gift. Even the idea that you could find a man to be given to is hardly an easy thought or concept to accept, much less em-brace. Experiences in our lives shape our ideas and beliefs. But experiences are also obstacles that need to be overcome. According to Romans 3:23, we all live in a fallen world and have all sinned so everything we experience is less than God-intended. The entire earth is groaning, waiting for the return of Jesus Christ (Romans 8:18-23). Thus, your experi-ence with man is also less than God intended from the start.

If we can acknowledge what God intended, perhaps, we can use it as the standard and allow the Word of God to give us a new vision and expectation. I have written a section called "Reclaiming the Lost Gift" on page 145. If you are having trouble sorting through all of this, I recommend that you pause and read that section before returning to this chapter.

When men and woman lose sight of the purpose of a woman, it is difficult to relate to one another as God intended.

Appreciating the Differences

Men and women are biologically and historically different from one another. Yet, we are interdependent on one another. Acknowledging differences does not mean denying equality. We must be different to praise and appreciate the differences in one another. This is how we ought to live our lives today.

There was a time when studying sex differences was thought to be pointless because sex was considered a social construct with the differences manufactured by culture. While there are social expectations of men and women, it is critical to acknowledge that these expectations are not only derived from civilizations and cultures, they are intentional creative differences from God.

Faith and fact prove that men and women are different.

God created the woman and the man to function differently. Because a woman's function differs from a man's, our biology and behavior will also differ. Here are a few ways scientific facts reveal God's intent when creating the woman functionally different.

Remember, the woman was created so that the man might not be *alone* or be *without help*. Women excel at being in relationships with others. Faith, facts, and professional evidence prove women are better communicators than men. It is also widely known that women tend to have greater verbal ability than men.[1] Cognitively, women have greater comprehension and better long-term memory than men.[2] As a counselor, I often observe that women seek to connect with others more so than men. We talk more about relationships with our husbands, children, family, friends, and everyone connected to us. We typically are the ones who immediately recognize a relationship problem or issue that exists, as we need to have a good relationship with those we are working with or supporting.

Another functional difference supported by behavioral science is that men tend to be more aggressive than women.[3] The thought is that men are quicker to become angry and display aggression as a survival instinct. In societies where survival is not a threat, men are considered more competitive than women. I believe this is important because it supports the idea of the woman as a nurturer, who is more likely to care for than compete with another. A 2015 study by Marco Giudice revealed that males scored high in dominance (assured-dominant) trait and low in the nurture (warm-agreeable) trait, repetitively.[4]

The socialization of men and woman is a real construct. And since we have given some examples which show that categorization happens on biological and psychological levels, I believe society only categorizes what is observed. I want to dismiss the idea that culture solely decides how a man and woman behaves.

Culture most certainly has an impact on gender roles. Yet, there are indisputable innate gender differences. This is where our creative God was purposeful in His distinction of the whole of humanity. Some sociologists support this idea as they observe young children who acknowledge differences before they are even taught they exist. Jean Stockard wrote in the book, *Handbook of the Sociology of Gender,* that children seem to become aware of gender difference even before they are culturally taught:

> "Long before children understand the nature of religious groups, occupations, or schooling, they realize that there are two sex groups and that they belong to one of these groups. The centrality of gender socialization also reflects the fact that our society, and all societies known to social scientists, are gendered.[5]

Men and women are different. This difference is complementary rather than something to compete against. Neither is better than the other. We both are interdependent on one another. Faith and fact reveal this truth. Whether married, single, divorced, or widowed, women embracing this truth will have better interaction with the men they choose to have in their lives. Such an idea empowers a woman to know her worth and wisely choose with whom she will connect.

Need for Caution and Discernment

We are given to men as a *treasured help, a champion, and a gift*. Discovering your abilities and talents helps you relate to a man and is critical before dating or marriage. While he is determining if you *can* help him, consider assessing if you are *willing* to help him. A man's vision and profession may not be conducive to how you want to live. This mismatch can create enormous turmoil in the relationship as you both want something different.

This is true for all of your male interactions, be it your father, brother, uncle, son, employer, and so on. This is especially true for a husband. Remember, God gave the command of dominion to both the male and female. When seeking a wife, a man looks for a woman adorned with the ability to help him rule and have dominion. He seeks a *gift* that can help him continue the work of God on the earth.

There is a common saying: "Before you marry, keep your eyes wide open." This implies the woman, as a gift, has a choice to whom she will give herself. The man asking the woman to marry him is all about his recognition of her gift and vowing he will view her as a *treasured help*. The woman's acceptance is about her agreement to *help* him. She agrees to be a *gift* to him. Seeking marriage is about you choosing whom you want to help and then you help.

Being a helpmate is not about serving without reciprocity. In healthy marital relationships, there is an exchange of care. The man loves the woman as he loves himself, and the wife seeks to respect her husband (Eph 5:33). Before marriage, a woman should assess the man and determine if he displays loving behaviors toward her and others in his life. Lying, cheating, stealing are all unloving behaviors and are not to be overlooked while dating. They point to deep issues that will return should the relationship continue. It is important to get this right before marrying. Once married, the focus for both the man and woman becomes how to give to the other. It is not about what we will receive from the other. Keeping a record of wrongs in a marriage does not produce a relationship where both prosper. Such situations usually leave both persons unsatisfied.

Because both men and women are flawed, relationships are never perfect or without struggles. Challenges will arise and may be the result of such things as gender differences or life transitions. These things can be worked through, as long as the desire is there. Sometimes people feel the gap is too wide between them to repair. Understanding the differences between men and women can help you navigate these issues as well as assist you in relating to the men in your life.

Two Types of Men

You may or may not be married. However, I imagine there is a man in your life that you are given to. A father, a brother, a son, a nephew – even a boss – all benefit from your interaction with them. Every man in our lives is different and may require different types of help. I dare say that there are only two types of men: godly and ungodly men. I pray as we look at the examples of two biblical women and the men they helped, you will be able to find yourself and find how to live in the truth of being a gift to a man.

Abraham and Sarah are a famous biblical couple. Together they waited on the promises of the Lord throughout their marriage. The story of Abraham and Sarah is found in Genesis chapters 12-25. It is worth the read. I will highlight how Sarah gifted the godly man, Abraham, and the challenges she had to face to do so.

We first meet the couple in Genesis 12 when God told Abram (later called Abraham) to leave his father's house and go to a land that God would show him. That required great faith and courage. Sarai (later called Sarah) followed her husband, understanding he did not have a plan that he could see. Abram immediately obeyed the Lord God by faith, and Sarai followed Abram. That was most certainly a gift as she trusted him with her life.

There were times Abraham feared and relied on Sarah's beauty to save him. There was also a time when Sarah became impatient and devised her plan to speed up God's promise to give her a child. Yet, Sarah remained a gift to her husband by following him as he followed God. He was not perfect, but he was reverent. She was not perfect but she was committed which made the difference in Sarah being a *treasured helper* to him.

You are most likely grateful for the man in your life who has visions of going places and doing big things. Sometimes he may have a map of how to get there, and other times, he may only have an idea. You may not always agree with him, but you still support him. This may even mean moving to a new city, draining a savings account, temporarily being the sole breadwinner or any other act of sacrifice for his vision. You want to trust that his relationship with God will lead you both to a place of peace and prosperity. Some days it takes all you have to give the gift of support. But you do it, being reminded that the man you are given to is one who is connected to God, and you trust God to guide him.

I want to encourage you that being in this place is not always easy. Yet, you have the grace to be there and are created to help. If you are like Sarai, then you have tried to do things in your own strength. You thought you knew better than your husband and attempted to make things happen. You may see things differently and you may be right. But God did not honor Abram because he had a wife that was right all the time. He honored Abram because Abram acknowledged and obeyed God. God and Abram forgave Sarai for her missteps. God will also forgive you and empower you to be a gift to the man who honors God.

Does your husband seek to honor God with his life? Even in his mistakes and what appears to be procrastination, is he praying and asking God for guidance? Just like you, Sarai was married to a godly man. Not a perfect man. Abram was intent on following God. And God saw this and was faithful. It was no doubt an adventure, yet Sarai, when yielded, not only had her name changed but also her plot in life. She had a son and more riches than she could have ever acquired on her own.

What about the men in your life who are not seeking the heart of God? How can you be a gift to them? In 1 Samuel 25:1-37, we find the story of Abigail and Nabal. Abigail was said to be an intelligent and beautiful woman; her husband was described as wealthy, but bad-tempered. Yet, under those circumstances, Abigail found a way to be a gift to him while she remained married to him.

I want to share this story from 1 Samuel 25. Please take the time to read it all so that you can grasp the picture of Abigail's life. It may be similar to yours.

Abigail was married to a man so mean that he was known for being "surly," or short-tempered. As if that were not enough, he would drink in excess until he would pass out. What made it worse was that Nabal was pretty well-off with resources. In short, Abigail was married to a man whom no one could reason. One day, his servants came to him and told him that David, a known warrior and the future king, requested some food and other resources from Nabal, whom David knew was rich. Nabal refused and disrespected David by referring to him as a runaway slave. Nabal's servants immediately enlisted the help of Abigail, Nabal's wife, and told her everything including their great concern that David would come and attack the estate. Abigail immediately gathered the items David requested and met him as he was coming to kill her husband. She shared her wisdom that the future king did not want to be known for shedding innocent blood. It was because of Abigail's intervention that David decided not to destroy the house of Nabal. He and his army turned around and continued their journey. Abigail, eager to share what just happened, returned home to find her husband too drunk to comprehend that she just saved his life (1 Samuel 25:2-37).

Abigail was able to save her husband's life with her intelligence, beauty, and courage. She knew exactly who Nabal was and who he was not. She covered him just as the woman covered her godly husband. He could trust her with his material wealth. He could trust her not to deceive him even in his drunkenness. She took care of his estate and his servants even when he would not. Different circumstances than the godly man yet, she was still a gift to the man Nabal.

I can imagine that day and many other days, Abigail was a gift to Nabal. She was not pleased with how he lived his life and at times felt threatened by his choices, yet, she was able to continue to be a gift to him. When he did not fulfill his role as a husband she gave no excuses to stop being a wife. She was always a gift to him until the day he died, which was shortly after the events of this story. God honors those who honor him and Nabal did not honor God in his life and his end resulted in sudden death.

The rest of the story indicated that God did not forget Abigail. Neither did David. Later in life, Abigail was rewarded for her faithfulness toward her husband. After Nabal's death, King David returned to marry this beautiful woman who saved her mean husband's life. David saw that Abigail was trustworthy, wise, well-kept, and productive. He saw her gift and treasured her. As you pray and share with God where you are, He will give you wisdom in how to live your life with an ungodly man.

Who is the ungodly man in your life? The mean one that you continue to save from the consequences of life? The proud man that believes his money buys him respect? Who is the drunk man in your life that you no longer try to reason with? Who is the serial cheater you painfully watch as he damages his soul? Know that God sees your efforts and your care for him. Be it a husband, brother, son, uncle, or boss, your quick thinking and courage can save his life. But also know that if things don't work out, you are *still a gift*. It is not easy to continue to care for someone who is not willing to care for themselves. Patience and faithfulness are required in all circumstances. If you are continuing to "help" an ungodly man, I pray for grace and peace be with you.

I realize the thought of a woman as a gift to both godly and ungodly men is an idea that angers many people today. I wrestled with the same issue, yet had to hold to the truth. God, infinite in wisdom, created this male-female dynamic. It is the sinful nature of mankind that creates barriers to believing God's Word. When both men and women lose sight of the purpose of the woman, it is difficult to relate to one another as God intended. When we return here, we can easily and willingly return to our *gift* status and accept being given to the man and never controlled by him.

The dysfunction now present between men and women does not have to be accepted any longer. While men contribute to undervaluing women, you and I have also contributed. The behavior of women, in general, has contributed to the current dysfunction between the sexes. As women, we can begin the paradigm shift by changing our behavior. We must name our contribution to the failed relationship between men and women before making a change.

Pointing the Blame

Feminism is a movement with a mission to help women relate differently to men. Some tenants of feminism are important to relay and promote today. The origins of feminism sought legal equality between men and women. The right to work, vote, obtain an education, and have religious expression are fundamental human rights everyone should enjoy, and they do not infringe on the rights of others. Feminism also arose to highlight women as victims who need rescuing from the mistreatment of men. Without a doubt, some men mistreat women with verbal, physical, economic, and other abuses. These things ought to change. I am grateful for the feminists who seek to make the lives of women better.

However, feminism from the 1960s seems to have morphed into an agenda no longer promoting equality or freedoms. Then there is what I call *radical feminism*, which is more of a browbeating approach that seeks to negatively label everyone, male and female, who does not agree with them. It is this latter form of feminism that has eroded the essence of womanhood and threatens the harmony between men and women. Radical feminists seem to want more than equality. The radical feminism approach would suggest they want upheaval to the centuries of interaction between men and women. This thought seems to want women to have dominion rather than share it with men. Unfortunately, this idea stuck as an effort to divide men and women.

Women who adopt this ideology abandon the role of being a *treasured helper* or a *gift* to the man. Rather they have become his accuser and his competitor. Such a mindset is constantly on the defensive looking to protect rather than give. Feminism claims to set the minds of women free. Yet, there is great apprehension and anger among all the women I consider radical feminists. It seems they are afraid of being taken advantage of or not appreciated for the things they do. They demand recognition for taking care of themselves. There is much emphasis on being *against* men, women, and children rather than being *with* men, women, and children.

I have seen and experienced the impact of adopting this feminist philosophy. I have discovered personally and professionally this is not the answer. While revealing injustices, feminism does not provide the answer to how women are to relate to men. We are given as a *treasured help, a champion, a gift*. We can fight this truth and live a lesser life or embrace this truth and learn the beauty of biblical womanhood. The beauty of biblical womanhood is that we are created equal yet different. Celebrating our differences does not diminish us. Rather it places us in a position as a precious, cherished, priceless *gift*.

Used vs. Useful

My challenge in relating to men started after I was married. In the marriage, I didn't want to live what I said I believed. I agreed that the woman is a gift to enhance the life of the man. However, the implementation called for self-sacrifice to which I did not agree. And, the more I fought against this idea that the woman is to nurture and care for those around her, the more dissatisfied I became. The more I tried to absolve myself of what I thought was unfair, the more dissatisfied I became. The unique part of me was no longer available to my family. I saw things my husband did not see. I knew things my husband did not know. Not that I am smarter than him but that I am *different* than him. I was no longer using my difference to enhance my family.

It was my differences that made a difference in his life and the life of our children. When I realized that whatever I left undone was something my family needed, I wanted to *fill the gap*. I realized the impact of my efforts amounted to even more than I was recognized. What I considered trivial was indeed an asset to the life of others. I did not always think this way. It was in those moments of taking a break that I begin to embrace how much I loved what I did. It is all I ever wanted to do. I simply needed to learn how to be a *gift* to the man.

My struggle with being given to the man was due to fear. I was afraid of being taken for granted or controlled. This was an idea planted in my head through the media of my generation. The images I saw and the songs I sang as a child all suggested that the woman is independent of the man. So, I was in my Christian marriage, seeking ways to be an individual even though I believed God made us one. The conflict within me was great, as I refused to believe neither statement was false.

I was double-minded. I had two different thoughts about the same thing. I struggled to abandon both beliefs, thinking one celebrated me and the other celebrated my marriage. Holding both the worldview and the truth of God's Word kept me in turmoil with myself and my husband.

---

*We cannot deny or change the truth
of the Word of God.*

Reframe

Even in the most unfortunate circumstances, we cannot deny the truth of God's Word, and we cannot change His truth. However, we can reframe it! Reframing is acknowledging that nothing changes about an idea or event, but rather the way I perceive the idea or event can change. We are not seeking to see God's Word differently, but rather the way it has been presented for centuries.

The reframe, a new perspective on an old idea, is that the woman is what God identified as the *need* of the man. The man needed the woman as it was "not good for man to be alone" (Genesis 2:18). The woman was necessary, relevant, a gift.

Embracing this truth about the woman, stopped the fight within me of caring for the men in my life. I relate to the man as his *treasured aid* because that is what I am, and admittedly, what I want to do. The very thing you seek to prove is already true about you. You *are* a gift!

When we reframe like this, it can help us relate differently to men. We no longer think of men wanting to be served and ourselves as women seeking to be their servants. We are then free to be all that we are created to be. There is much freedom knowing that before we speak or act, we are already a gift. Being confident in this truth impacts our speech and behavior. When we are not convinced of this truth, we use our speech and behavior to demand value.

When you understand your design and purpose at creation, you will know that what you contribute to the community of people around you is great. God gifted the woman to the man. This man held all of mankind within him. You are a gift right where you are to all the men, women, and children that surround you.

The God-Man

Jesus Christ is the Son of God. He came in the image of a man to save the world. His salvation is divine, and He is the bridge between the divine and mankind. Jesus Christ is the God-man to whom we are all given. He is the perfect man who will never let us down. Connecting with the God-man is necessary to help us relate to the men in our lives. He is the One we trust to be our everything. He is the One who will never fail us. Trusting Him is necessary to build trust in mankind. If you do not know the God-man as your Savior, please learn more about Jesus Christ. To help you with this, see the section entitled, "Getting to Know Your Creator" on page 143.

Wait, What If I Don't Want To?

Some women do not desire to relate to a man as a husband or as a sexual partner. These women refer to themselves as many things including asexual, lesbian, or simply disinterested. There are several reasons why a woman may arrive at this conclusion about herself. This begs me to ask: If the woman who desires male companionship must embark on self-exploration, how much more the woman who is disinterested in connecting with a man at all?

There are women of all ages and cultures who express this lack of desire to relate to a man. Not having this desire is only a symptom and nothing of great concern. What is more important to grasp is the reason behind it – the reason *why*. This question is not meant to be offensive, but instead an assumption that you have completed self-exploration on the issue. Being able to answer this question would suggest that you have considered both internal and external factors in your choice to relate to men differently than outlined in Genesis 2:22.

If you have not explored this issue, I highly recommend you work with a biblical counselor or Christian therapist to explore and process this decision. As a woman, you are intended to be the best gift you can be. Knowing yourself and understanding your choices, refines your gift-giving.

Seeing yourself as a gift to a man impacts how you relate to the opposite sex. If you find value in what you bring, you will insist on being valued. Therefore, it is critical to reassess your thoughts and beliefs about womanhood. Getting this wrong could last a lifetime and pass from generation to generation. Getting it right can change the world.

Reflecting on Yourself as a Gift to Man

Take a few moments to pause and reflect on what you've read about womanhood. Record below what God reveals about your heart and the truth He shares with you:

1. What are some differences between men and women that you most appreciate?

2. What abilities and talents do you think you currently possess that could help a man?

3. How do you think your behaviors are a gift to others?

4. Do you have any behaviors that devalue you and your gift?

5. Do you think a man chooses a wife? Explain.

Do you think a woman chooses a husband? Explain.

6. What should your spouse display for you to want to help him?

"I have no greater joy than to hear my children are walking in the truth."

3 John 4

5

You Are a Gift to Children

Motherhood is an experience. I dare say above an experience, motherhood is an attitude. It is the welcomed posture of self-sacrifice. This attitude is found in women with the experience of raising children and women who love children. A mother is a woman who willingly denies herself so that the children in her life can benefit. This selfless attitude is what has allowed civilizations to continue since the beginning of time. In this chapter, when I refer to a mother, I am referencing any woman with a selfless attitude toward the children around her.

A mother is any woman with a selfless attitude toward the children around her.

Created to Care for Children

In discussing womanhood, I want to emphasize the weight of the mother's role. She often provides the foundation that nurtures the basic needs of the children. I certainly do not intend to overlook the contributions of fathers; they are critical in the development of children. I want to be clear that there are fathers who expertly care for their children, however, that happens at a slower pace and with much intention and effort.

Women are the first caretakers of children as we carry them in our bodies. From the moment we are pregnant we become responsible for that child and the care needed to help that child become the best adult begins immediately. As we watch what we are eating and the level of strenuous activity we engage in, it impacts the development of a child.

Development continues outside of the womb and is still largely dependent upon the woman. The greatest gift a woman can give a child is the gift of faith. When we share our faith in God and live out our faith, children have a model to grasp and a hope to hold. When we live a lifestyle of faith we help our children develop theirs. When we do not, we hinder them from believing in God.

Women are equipped to care for children.

As mothers, we are our children's first point of contact in learning about this world. God's Word promises that if you and I "start children off in the way they should go, even when they are old they will not turn from it" (Proverbs 22:6). It is our spiritual obligation to reinforce the Word of God in our children's lives. We best communicate our faith through our behaviors and how we care for our children.

The Bible discusses how a child without correction disgraces his mother (Proverbs 29:15). The child cannot correct himself. The mother must join in with her husband to teach her child, otherwise, she will experience shame. We primarily teach our children when they are present with us. Spending intentional time with our children is critical in nurturing and guiding them into the truth of God's Word.

As women, we also teach our children about how to relate to others. Remember this is a large part of why we were created. After teaching them about God, we teach them about others and the rest of the world. Both faith and fact agree on the tremendous influence of a woman in the life of a child.

Committed to the Care of Children

Ultimately, women were created to care for children. Personal experience, faith, and research reveal that women are natural nurturers and care for children not because society says so but because we are equipped to do so. The study of anthropology proves that women and children are often coupled together. For centuries women were thought to not only deliver the children but also nurture them into independence. Whether it is her children or children in the community, the woman is equipped to care for the next generation.

As the media encourages women to live independently of others, the negative impact is readily seen in society. Marriage and family researchers are seeking to turn their findings into policy because of the wide-spread impact of women no longer caring for children. It is a silent trend that has a significant impact on children and society.

The Overseas Developmental Institute (ODI) uses research to create change for international development and humanitarian issues. In 2016, ODI's mission and conclusion about childcare confirmed the power of a woman's care for children and the impact when it is absent. Their findings are best shared in their words:

There is an evident 'care gap' in many countries, and care responsibilities are having negative impacts on mothers and other [caregivers]. A lack of care is also damaging children where mothers are pushed to their limits by the twin demands of caring and providing for their families... Today's care realities are sharply different from those of just a generation ago. Owing to shifts in women's labour market engagement, improvements in girls' education, increases in migration and urbanization, and changes to family structure, women need more external support for care. While women have tried to go it alone, as reflected in time-use statistics indicating that they work far more hours each day than men, the tens of millions of young children around the world left with inadequate care point to the untenable trade-offs that many women are facing, especially in low-income contexts...The costs borne by women and children – and indeed society more broadly – will surely continue to grow if governments and development partners alike do not take urgent action.[1]

Faith and fact point to the necessity of the woman's gift in caring for children. This is not just an old idea that needs to change. Changing it will impact all of society, and we may not know how to account for the immediate repercussions. Again, a woman sacrifices greatly to care for children. Your attention will shift from your needs to theirs. This does not mean we give up our lives entirely. It means we filter our lives through the needs of the children around us. We become more conscious of how our decisions impact them. We begin to make decisions that are in the best interest of our families, which means our interests are, at times, delayed, or denied. Denying yourself or being selfless does not sound appealing. However, it is a function of womanhood and how we as women move on the earth.

The gift of the woman to children requires both self-sacrifice and self-care. As I mentioned earlier, it is difficult to develop another person and not care for yourself. For a woman to give to children or others, she must have something to offer. Whether the children in your influence are near or far, you have something to give them. A smile, a hug, food, comfort, or something more means so much coming from you. Though you may tire, the gift you bring is unique and needed by the children around you.

The Female Presence

The impact of a woman's touch in a child's life is also critical. Children who have a female touch in their lives are more likely to become healthy adults. Without this touch, children grow into adults who focus so much on finding worth, that their purpose is delayed. It is difficult to live as God intended when one is not convinced of his or her worth. As a result, children who lack a "mother's touch" grow up engaging in and accepting unhealthy behaviors from others. Healthy children can become healthy adults and it starts with the touch of a woman.

The benefits of a woman's touch on a child go beyond the duty of feeding, bathing, and clothing. These are essential, and hopefully, things every child will have one day. How a woman completes her everyday tasks affects a child's physical, emotional, and spiritual development. Countless research shows that the amount or lack of nurturing children receive early in life impacts them well into adulthood. Here are just a few benefits children receive from the gift of the woman.

1. Children need someone to invest in them as it helps promote their physical development.

Research suggests that a woman's nurturing of a child can assist with a child's brain development. Children who have nurturing homes have a larger hippocampus, which is responsible for memory and emotion. If a mother imprints loving memories in a child's brain, it impacts the way the brain grows but also the emotional stability of the child.[2] Ultimately, these children perform better in school and the job market. The absence of the mother also impacts the brain. Erica Kosmar, author of *Being There: Why Prioritizing Motherhood in the First Three Years Matters*, attributes a mother's absence to the increase in the trend of ADHD, aggression, and social disorders found in children. Women who can protect children from stress early in life encourage children to learn resiliency as the attachment bond helps them feel safe. Ultimately, Kosmar believes the mother's presence is a protectant to the child and creates a feeling of safety. This sense of safety allows for healthy emotional development.

> What is vital for both the short-term and long-term well-being of your child is your emotional presence. And I want to stress that without physical presence-if you were not with your child, you cannot be emotionally present. And just as the time spent with your

child has long-term benefits, the lack of that essential connection can have lifelong repercussions.[3]

2. Children who grow up with nurturing women are less likely to experience depression and other mental health issues.

When a woman chooses to care for you, it makes you believe you have worth and value. This belief continues throughout childhood and is displayed even as an adult. Mothers are the ones who encourage their children and speak words that shape a child's self-image. This happens both positively and negatively. Being mentally and emotionally healthy is important as a woman because you indirectly teach your children how to handle emotions. Brigham Young University studied emotional control and problem solving of mothers through a questionnaire. They found that mothers with greater emotional control and executive functioning (problem-solving skills) are less likely to develop children with behavioral problems.[4] This may seem obvious, but it is also a challenge for us to take responsibility for ourselves so that we can be responsible for others. Children are directly impacted by how we manage our own lives. They will learn and later imitate what we display.

3. Women are wired to help teach children the necessary relationship skills to obtain their needs.

Children are demanding people. Their needs are plenteous and their desires unending. Taming the innate selfishness of children requires patience and endurance. Remember, the woman was designed to relate and nurture. Her gift begins with the family and spreads to the community of the children she encounters. Without the touch of a woman, children have difficulty with socialization and developing healthy relationships.

We have noted earlier that women are created as relational beings. We seek to connect with people and engage in ways that promote unity. This is our general approach to every person we meet. Children learn to approach others as companions and not immediate competitors because of the touch of a woman.

This is true even regarding romantic relationships. What a mother displays in choosing partners is replicated in the life of her child. A 24-year study revealed mothers with weak romantic relationships passed similar relationship identities down to their offspring: "results suggest that the transmission of poor marriageable characteristics and relationship skills from mother to child may warrant additional attention as a potential mechanism through which the number of partners continues across generations."[5] Ultimately, the study supports my earlier premise that women are the keepers of society. What we do has an impact on the next generation.

How you display womanhood before children matters. When you are intentional about this, the outcome is clear that your presence is a *gift* to the children, and they are free to grow into healthy adults.

Shifting

When I married my husband, we ran an egalitarian home. That means we were all equal to contribute to the home based on needs rather than gender. He and I both cooked and washed clothes. After the children arrived, there was this unspoken shift where we both began to address different needs. He started working more, and I started caring for the house and children more. Although swift, my shift into motherhood was not without its challenges. Within the first year of having my son, my husband and I were sitting in marriage counseling. My worldview and biblical view of womanhood were on a collision course that I could not prevent. I was struggling as a woman, a wife, and a mother.

There we sat in the counselor's office, desperately seeking answers to relieve the strain and pressure in our marriage. The counselor asked us to perform an interesting exercise. This exercise challenged my image of motherhood in a way that remains with me today. She asked us to envision ourselves paddling together in the boat of life. Both of our hands were at work fulfilling dominion as God purposed. Then I became pregnant and gave birth; as a result, the boat slowed down. We both were still paddling, but now I was holding a baby in one hand while paddling with the other. I quickly responded, "Yes, that is why both of my arms are tired." This attitude began to infiltrate everything I did in the home, and I became resentful having to care for the family.

My frustration grew every day as I realized my life was not becoming easier, but more difficult. I was becoming accustomed to addressing the needs of my husband and now there was another person who needed my attention. I was feeling exhausted and overlooked. I did not have any new ideas but continued to rehearse the pain and discomfort I was feeling. I needed help and began to look outside of myself for help. I began to look to my God and other women.

This period of exploration helped me discover what I was doing is what women do. All the women I talked to emphasized the joy they experienced in caring for others. They never said it was easy. And they did express being tired at times. But ultimately, they were grateful for the opportunities they had to care for children and see the hand of God work through those situations.

Over time, I gravitated to a place of helping my husband while still caring for our children. I enjoyed watching my children grow and learn, and when they were not around, I missed them. Being with my children was difficult at times, but exactly what I wanted. I finally understood the message our marriage counselor tried to convey with the boat exercise. My purpose in life did not change when I married and became a wife and mother. I was fulfilling it, albeit in a way I never imagined. I was the help my husband needed, the nurturer my children needed, and the asset my business and community needed. My pace was slower, but my purpose was still evident. When I stopped fighting my expanded role and began to embrace it, my relationship with my husband and children changed for the better. While I am still growing in this area, I am more confident that what I am doing is exactly what I want to do.

Your Irreplaceable Value

As a gift to children, you are valuable and irreplaceable. A mother's selflessness offers children the first step to wholeness and becoming productive citizens. It is part of her design and purpose to be a gift to children. Being with your children is about prioritizing them and their wellbeing. All women can be a gift to children. You are equipped to do so, too. It is up to you to choose the level of impact you will have on a child's life.

Again, regardless of your relation to children, your touch is necessary to a child's life. You are built to impart something to the next generation. As you become more and more convinced that you are a gift, you will become more intentional about how you engage the next generation. When you influence a child for Christ, you give that child the greatest gift he could ever receive – the opportunity to know a Savior.

What if I Don't Have Children?

I realize not all women can have biological children. Some may be medically unable to bear children but are truly gifts to them, as the inclination to care for children is present. These women have so much love to give, and many times seek out ways to nurture children through foster care, adoption, children-focused careers, volunteering, mentoring, and more.

My prayer is that if you do not have biological children, you can continue to know your value and your special place in the lives of children around you. There are likely nieces, nephews, godchildren, students, neighbors, and others to whom you can selflessly give your time and resources. What you bring is an invaluable gift that encourages children toward wholeness. You are needed to create imprints in the life of a child or the children that surround you.

I am also aware that some women have no desire for children, and that is okay, too. This lack of desire could be a result of your personality, upbringing, life experiences, or simply counting the cost of parenting. It is not uncommon or any less of your womanhood not to have this desire. The important thing, again, is to discover *why* there is not a desire. I frequently tell my clients to summarize their decisions in one sentence. Doing so requires them to think about their reasons and filter through them. It requires significant reflection and evaluation but allows them to search inward and identify the core or source of their reasoning.

Sometimes after doing this exercise, people change their answers about their life decisions. Sometimes they do not. You can do this exercise and not develop a desire for children. However, doing the work means you are more convinced and have an even greater conviction that not having children is the right answer for you. What tends to happen is that you still find something to nurture and a place for you to offer yourself as a gift. Doing so is what makes you undoubtedly a woman, a *gift*.

Reflecting on Yourself as a Gift to Children

Take a few moments to pause and reflect on what you've read about womanhood. Record below what God reveals about your heart and the truth He shares with you:

1. As a child, who was your first example of womanhood?

2. In what ways do you think she exemplified womanhood?

3. What do you believe is your impact on children?

4. Who are the children in your life currently benefiting from your gift?

5. How would you define self-sacrifice?

6. How would you define self-care?

7. Is it possible for a woman to both display self-sacrifice and self-care? If so, how?

8. How have you seen the positive impact of a mother figure in a child's life?

9. How have you seen the impact of the absence of a mother figure?

10. If your desire is not to raise children (or your circumstances haven't allowed it), identify your nurturing behaviors in the space below, and ask God for opportunities to use them.

---

*"For a woman to say "I am a gift,"
is for her to acknowledge and accept
that her individuality is unique
only in community with others."*

Tina Taylor

Wife, Mother, Counselor

6

You Are a Gift to Your Community

The design of a woman in society is to cultivate healthy relationships among her sphere of influence. She is created with the purpose of helping and relating. Relating to others is the best way for a woman to fulfill her dominion. God is a relational being. He seeks to be in a relationship with mankind and empowers women to reflect this image.

Thus far, I've defined womanhood in the context of community. Whereas personal identity highlights how you are different than the whole, a community is needed to emphasize individuality.

As a pillar to society, a woman's soft touch is necessary to promote peace and comfort in towns and cities across the world. I have discovered that my impact begins with the daily choices I make regarding the people and situations I touch. There is nothing we do that is insignificant or small. We are all needed, and our expressions of womanhood are gifts to our communities and our world. When we embrace our role and the importance of it, we are less likely to see ourselves independent of others. Let us observe how looking beyond yourself and serving others not only sustains society but also brings us joy.

Serving the Community

Take a moment to look around and reflect on the world. You will see the impact of women and how necessary we are to all of humanity. As we care for one another, it enables the human race to continue and shows forth the love of God. What we do directly helps others and indirectly helps us.

There are so many different community groups you can join to serve and connect with other women. I want to acknowledge and thank the many women-focused groups that demonstrate the message of this book. I highly encourage you to seek out long-standing women's organizations where you can continue interacting with other women. Together you can gift your community with love and care. Having a group of women to serve alongside also encourages our commitment and gives us opportunities to encourage one another.

God created you with unique gifts to your circle of influence. When you are not present, something is missing. Something necessary. Something significant. While you attempt to be an individual, remember that you were created to be in relationship—with God and with others. As you remain connected to God, He will help you to live your purpose as a *treasured help* to the men, women, and children in your community.

Consider intentionally seeking out different community organizations that can benefit from your talents and abilities. This maybe your church but also can include other nonprofits that benefit humanity. Some people like to serve and help others. Yet, they do this without the light of Christ. How much more can Christ be glorified and lifted when we serve out of our relationship with Him? When we go to these places and allow our light to shine, others will want to know "How do you do it?" Our service offers an opportunity to show Christ on the earth.

You may be asking yourself, *How am I to be a gift to my house, my friends, my family, and now strangers? I do not have enough time in my day to do all of this.* I understand how this may seem impossible. However, as a virtuous woman, you allow the Spirit of God to lead you and direct your steps. God created you as a woman and know that He created you for the capacity to care for others. We do not care for everyone at the same time. As we follow Christ, we will be able to look up and see that He has enabled us to care for those He has given us to. Following Him and you will do all these things and more.

Faith and scientific fact confirm that women are care-givers. Your personal experience will also reveal that you are able to give to others at a different pace than you may even be aware. Consider taking inventory of your life over the past year. Did you find that you gave out more than you even realized? If so, then you probably are eager to engage in self-care. If not, I hope you are motivated to engage more with others so that you, too, can share in the joy of nurturing and developing others.

The Importance of Community

Community is very much about the place where you dwell and the people who occupy that place. Community also includes other people with whom you share a close relationship. These relationships help foster a sense of belonging but also growth. When we allow ourselves to connect with other women, we can develop a shared space for each of our unique gifts. We can inspire one another to live a life on purpose and according to our design. When this community of other women is absent in our lives, there exists a place of loneliness within us. This has been my experience.

As you think about your community, do you find that you have other women you can encourage and those who can encourage you? We are all engaged in the community around us, and we can have an even greater impact when we do things together.

Encouraging One Another

A woman's capacity to form relationships help people stay connected and build community on the earth. We not only need each other, we were created for one another! It is impossible to explore who we are as women without examining it in the context of how we relate to men, children, and even other women. While you are being a gift to the individuals around you, may you also receive the gift of other women in your life.

When women gather together, we have so much to offer one another. When we are intentional about the exchange, there can be so many great things revealed in our lives and the lives of others. Sitting around sharing experiences can improve the lives of the women present. Engaging in women's circles allows us to be reminded and encouraged that we are not in this alone. It also provides an opportunity for us to encourage one another.

From a faith perspective, the Bible tells us that it is more blessed to give than to receive (Acts 20:35). As women, we are always giving out, yet it is amazing how we still find ways to give to those outside of our homes and our families. No matter how much time we give when we serve the community, we have an opportunity to show the love of God. And any effort we provide is an opportunity to change the life of another person. This is a spiritual truth that serving others is to our benefit as women.

In Titus 2, the Bible instructs how women can serve the community. The focus of this book of the Bible is how believers are to live in community with one another. Titus 2:3-4 encourages the intentional gathering of older women with younger women so the image of the biblical woman continues from generation to generation:

"the older women likewise, that they be reverent in behavior, not slanderers, not given to much wine, teachers of good things—that they admonish the young women to love their husbands, to love their children,…"

I love that these verses acknowledge that younger women need to be taught about womanhood. Although we talked about all the innate qualities that make us a gift, the gifts still require training, correction, and at times loving rebuke. In allowing another woman to speak into your life as such, helps you stay honest with God, others, and yourself. Remember the verse in Galatians 6:2 that tells us to carry the burdens of one another? The verse that follows tells us, "if anyone thinks himself something when he is nothing, he deceives himself"(verse 3). Having a sisterhood where you are celebrated and corrected is necessary to help paint the picture of your true beauty. As you reflect the image of God within you, you are being a gift to those you influence.

This charge not only indicates that God knew we would need help, but also that we would have to be intentional about carrying out the role of a woman as God intended. He knew we would be distracted by the ways of the world. The intentional teaching of older godly women is necessary for our community. It is part of becoming a woman.

Generations of women are lost, without examples of biblical womanhood to follow.

Psychologically and biologically, when women are together, these moments boost our emotional and mental states, impacting our overall health. Scientific studies of female friends highlight that the chemical bonding hormone of oxytocin is released when women engage with one another.[1] Oxytocin helps reduce levels of stress as women feel comforted and not alone when dealing with stressful life events, even with challenges like cancer. This fact supports our faith practice of helping to bear one another's burdens.

While we need each other, there are specific reasons that prevent women from joining women's circles. Aggression, gossip, jealousy, and anger management are a few reasons identified in Jacqueline Mroz's book, *Girl Talk: What Science Can Tell Us About Female Friendships.* These behaviors are found among women, yet the benefits of bonding with other women are greater than the drawbacks of sin. Mroz concluded that women still need friendships while working on overcoming these issues with social skill training.[2] As you and I continue to seek Christ and walk in wisdom, we do not have to avoid female friendships but rather can model biblical friendships where Christ is our focus and we can grow together in Him.

Going at it Alone

In times past, mankind thrived in communal living. This was a time when everyone worked together and shared all things in common. In this environment, women gathered over daily tasks, relating, and teaching one another. Conversations and wisdom were passed down from one generation to the next. It was where grandmothers, mothers, aunts, and sisters all became mentors by telling, sharing, and showing other women how to live.

As mankind began to advance, families shared property but no longer living spaces. With further advancement, families have become so dispersed we are losing both life lessons and emotional attachments.

As you journey through this book, I hope you fostered new relationships with women. Taking time to encourage one another in our created roles can help us embrace where we are and what we are called to do. This can provide greater clarity and encouragement in accepting the truth about womanhood. Telling our stories and hearing the stories of others can affirm us in our life choices. This dialogue can also present the option to make better life choices; that alone could save future generations.

With the demands of today's woman, she is managing her immediate family, working, and engaging community interests. These are all challenging and difficult tasks to undertake; because of this, engaging with other women has become less of a priority. Many women have a community of other women. They are experiencing the joys of this community. But there also remains many women who are developing their expression of womanhood, alone.

Maybe you are like me and have great women surrounding you, yet you feel unsure about your expression of womanhood. Or your story could be that you did not have any women to model in your life and now you need help to form a picture of who you want to be.

You Only Need a Few

I was a sophomore in college when I knew I would write a book. The idea was birthed after having dinner with my roommate and her mother. Out of nowhere, I asked this older woman who was of a higher economic status, and a different culture than me, her advice on being a woman. I will never forget her response, as it seemed to speak to what was lacking within me. Her response somehow revealed my wounds and soothed them at the same time. She told me, "You only need a few friends. When you find them, keep them close." It was at that moment I realized there was so much to learn, and so much more I wanted to know.

I was a loner with many friends. You know, the type that attends a party and speaks to everyone there, but leaves early. I was just social enough to engage but distant enough to leave early. This woman who gave me the advice to keep close friends close seemed so different from me, yet she saw my need and had an answer for me. It was an answer I am still seeking to live out 20 years later.

I remember looking at her and seeing something new: An unfamiliar expression that embodied this beautiful woman and her story. I left dinner, thinking I would interview women from diverse backgrounds and collect wise guidance for life. I wish I could blame the busyness of life with overshadowing this notion and preventing me from accomplishing my goal. However, I realized that I lost the treasure of this truth just as quickly as I gained it. What I discovered was soon lost to what I feared, and I again became a loner amid the crowd.

More than two decades later, the discovery that I only need a few close friends has never left me. I have been longing for this place where I can be fully seen and loved by others. It is this place that was lost when I was a child.

It is amazing how people can easily create wounds in our lives. The adult in me knows God is a healer, and His love through people can cover the wounds we receive from others. This truth, at times, collides with this little girl who is uncertain if the people who say they will be there will indeed be there.

The Impact of Childhood Pain

The effect of my pain, I know, impacts my expression of being a woman. As a counselor who hears the stories from women of various backgrounds, I know this to be true for others as it is for me. *Pain prevents us from being the best we can be.* Whether we experience physical pain or emotional pain, they both impede the purpose of our lives. With God's help, we can learn to live beyond the pain.

Pain is so prevalent in the world today. I see it so clearly among women today who have lost their identity because of not understanding the true expression of womanhood. They walk around, emphasizing their accomplishments and achievements while disrespecting or disregarding others.

This leaves generations of women lost, without examples of real womanhood to follow. I had many superb women to emulate, yet I struggled with finding my own expression. How much more the young lady without someone to model real womanhood before her.

Overcoming pain is essential to personal healing and building a community. It is tough to connect with people when you see them as causing pain, both emotional and physical. This perception will cause you to create walls that keep you safe, but also keep others out.

Breaking the Trend

I felt so alone until my mentor, Margo Parsons, came into my life and invited me to enter into a mentoring relationship with her. She offered to share life with me, giving me what she had and challenging me to give to others as well. The result of her invite started me on a different path in womanhood, one where I am extending my community of women.

Having someone alongside you to encourage you in your efforts makes a difference. Whatever we are nurturing in the community, we will need the support of others to help us keep going. Life can bring so many different challenges to oppose our efforts to develop and maintain healthy families and community relationships. However, in our community of other women, we can find a cheerleader to cheer us on and a taskmaster to keep us accountable for the work.

It is only through the combination of affirmation and accountability in life that we experience mental and emotional maturity. You and I need another person to comfort us but also confront us. Mental and emotional maturity is an intentional process. You must lean into the process to mature in your gift. It is through truth and love given in community that we display the biblical expression of womanhood.

I have come to believe that I can learn something from everyone if I seek to listen. I believe this so much that I am encouraging you to do the same. Listen to the stories of the women around you. You may have the same path or the exact opposite, but you can encourage and strengthen one another along the way. The women before us had it right to come together and encourage one another. When we do this we are more able to carry out the different tasks assigned to each of us.

We each are needed to make our homes and communities thrive. The differences we bring can complement one another and advance the places where we live and serve. I hope that you can grab your "squad" and together make an impact in your communities.

Consider how your expression of womanhood could advance others. These and other opportunities are available at www.justserve.org.

- **After-school tutor**
- **Write or make cards for hospitalized persons**
- **Assist the elderly**
- **Sponsor a college student**
- **Serve meals**
- **Lead a Bible study**
- **Be a court advocate for children**
- **Be a hospice companion**
- **Write or make cards for deployed troops**
- **Volunteer at a school**
- **Babysit**
- **Tutor homeless children**
- **Become a language interpreter**
- **Crochet items for children in foster care**
- **Help with literacy for adult learners**
- **Donate clothing**
- **Participate in community clean up**
- **Mentor others**
- **Transport the elderly or disabled**
- **Sit and talk with a widow**
- **Visit nursing homes**
- **Organize a yard sale and donate to charity**
- **Volunteer at a hospital**
- **Volunteer at your church**

Reflecting on Yourself as a Gift to Your Community

Take a few moments to pause and reflect on what you've read. Record below what God reveals about your heart and the truth He shares with you:

1. Who are the people in your community? List below the people you care for outside of your immediate family.

2. What has been your role in your community?

3. Have you ever considered your role as your *gift* to others? Why or why not?

4. Who are the women in your life who can celebrate with you? List them here. (If you don't have any, write the names of women you'd like to have that kind of relationship with.)

5. Is there at least one other woman in your life who can correct you? If yes, whom? If no, why not?

6. If you are a mentor, have you been mentored yourself? Yes or No.

7. List any women's organization you are part of (or are considering joining).

"My life is made sweeter by what I can do for others...I am fulfilled watching the life of others improve because of my influence."

Susan Wilson

Wife, Mother, Community Leader

7
What Next?

Here you are at the end of this journey. Thank you for being engaged and committed to finishing this book. You have identified the influences in your life that lead you to the ideal of womanhood. You worked through the creation story and explored the Bible for practical examples of womanhood. I hope you were able to dismantle any false images you may have had and allow God to help you rediscover the beauty of being a woman. As you embraced this truth and looked at all of your relationships, I trust you discovered your purpose is to be a gift to those within your sphere of influence.

Now that you've seen the beauty of biblical womanhood and all that you are created to do are you excited to live it out in a way that impacts everyone around you?
In the first half of the book, we identified what we believed was womanhood based on the media and personal experience. We journeyed together through Scripture to identify the true design and intent of womanhood. Remember, the woman was created as a *treasured helper*, *a gift* from God

given to the man and mankind. She is created to nurture others through relationships and the use of her talents and abilities. We completed the goal of the book in defining womanhood while allowing individual expression.

In addition to embracing biblical womanhood, another goal of the book was to complete the book with at least one other woman. Sharing your story and listening to the stories of others is how we build relationships, knowledge, and community. I highly encourage you to continue asking questions of one another. Continue learning about how other women have survived as you consider the way you want to live.

Here at the end of the book, I hope you have both observed and experienced the gift of womanhood. Gaining certainty in your purpose and design will undoubtedly yield productive fruit. It is my sincere desire that the time spent reading this book and reflecting on its questions has prompted you to act.

What you have experienced has only been a precursor to what you can continue to enjoy in your life, should you desire more. You have started a good thing; it will require intentionality to keep it going. I have provided a recommended reading list to help continue the conversation and discovery of the potential God placed within you.

You are a gift, a treasured helper to the people around you.

I titled this book *I Am A Gift* as an affirmation for you. Declaring "I Am a Gift" promotes individuality only within the context of community. It is acknowledging that the Great "I AM" created "A woman" as "A Gift." *You are a gift, a treasured helper valuable to those around you.* This is the overarching message communicated throughout this book.

Now it is your turn to be a gift to others.

Now What?

- **Pray. Pray. Pray**. Pray often. There is no way you and I can be what God intended without His help. Sin has entered the world and seeks to overtake us. The daily images we see contradict what God says about us and intended for us. To combat the attacks in your mind and spirit, you must stay connected with God.
- **Change your thoughts.** When your thoughts change, your behavior will change. Accept the truth of God's Word in that He created a treasured help, the woman champion. Embracing this idea will aid your attitude in caring for the people you love. Declare "I Am a Gift" as you approach your daily activities.
- **Embrace (or find) a group where you can grow.** Proverbs 27:17 says, "As iron sharpens iron, So a man [or woman] sharpens the countenance of his [or her] friend." The company you keep shapes

your character. Find a woman who can mentor (and sharpen) you, a woman you can mentor (and sharpen), and peer support where you exchange the ups and downs of life. Finding these three spaces is imperative to your continued growth as a woman. You may already have identified these special women in your life, but naming them as such will increase the value to the women in your circle. Remember, it takes time and intentionality to build these relationships.

I am so glad that we reached the end together. Well, maybe this is just the beginning as we take our new mindset back into our everyday lives. Let's see if our change will stir change in the people we love and care for. I believe it will. And I am convinced that as you care for others, God will allow others to care for you too. Keep your eyes open for all the ways God will aid you to live out what He purposed for your life. God loves His daughters and made each of us a gift. *You are a gift!*

Reflecting on Your Purpose

Take a few moments to pause and reflect on what you've read. Record below what God reveals about your heart and the truth He shares with you:

1. What do you want to do differently now that you've read this book?

2. Think of a mentor or another important woman in your life. Consider sharing with her in a phone call or hand-written letter what you most admire about her expression of womanhood.

3. Consider making a list of the significant women in your life, both past and present. In what ways can you honor them?

A Prayer for Commitment

Father, at the start of this book, my outlook on womanhood was based on a lot of things. A lot of different things. I admit I was double-minded and uncertain about the expression of womanhood You wanted to display within me. I thought I knew, but Father, through reflecting on my thoughts and reflecting on your Word, I realize something was missing. My thoughts were not Your thoughts, and my ways were not your ways (Isaiah 55:8-9). I ask that You forgive me.

I also ask You to renew my mind so that my heart can be set free. You did just that. You renewed my mind so that I might know Your perfect will concerning me as a woman. Thank You for being faithful to Your Word and for giving me the truth to help set me free. I understand that You created me to fill a need, and Your intentions for me have not changed. You have given me the faith and facts to prove that I am my best in relationship with others. I am a treasured helper. I admit that I am at times scared that the gift within me may be taken for granted or even abused. I ask that You lead me. I pray Your Holy Spirit guide me in relating to others. May my life be filled with good works so that men, women, and children will glorify you in heaven (Matthew 5:16).

Father, I now ask that You help me continue to pursue You and Your Truth. I understand I can only remain a gift when connected to the gift-giver, You (John 15:4). Help me to continue to live out Your Word which encourages me to share in the lives of others. Help me to hide this word in my heart, that I may be found pleasing to You (Psalm 119:11). In Jesus' Name, Amen.

"My purpose here is to help someone. Therefore, I try to do all the good I can while I can.

Sylvia Frazier

Wife, Aunt, Educator

You are a gift,
a treasured helper valuable to
those around you.

Love Tina

Getting to Know Your Creator

When we get to know our Creator, we can know ourselves and return to His intent and purpose for our lives. No matter how far we have left our purpose and design, there is good news: The Gospel of Jesus Christ and His sacrifice of love can reach and rescue us.

God believes you are so valuable that He gave His only son, Jesus, to die for all the wrong you have done. Jesus, in love, willingly left heaven to come to suffer and die for you and me. He later was resurrected and ascended into heaven, where He now sits on the throne next to God. He sits there, being a mediator between you and God. When you accept Jesus as your Savior, your sins, or wrongdoings, are forgiven once and for all (Mark 2:8-11; Romans 10:1-13). If you should happen to sin again, confess your sins, God is consistently merciful and will always forgive you (1 John 1:9). He thinks you are just that valuable.

When we accept the love of God through Christ Jesus, we can walk with God daily. Our hearts are inclined to receive Him and His Word. As if dying on the Cross was not enough, Jesus, understanding our human nature: 1) gave us His Spirit; and 2) intercedes for us.

When we accept Jesus into our hearts, the Holy Spirit comes into our lives to teach and comfort us. It is through the Holy Spirit that we learn God's Word and find comfort in our times of need. The Holy Spirit also helps us walk as Jesus walked on the earth. Through the fruit of the Holy Spirit, we can relate to God and one another (Galatians 5:22-23). The Holy Spirit enables us to live out true womanhood.

You may have heard of God, Jesus, and the Holy Spirit as the Trinity or the God-head. Maybe you have not and are not sure of how it all works, but one thing you know is that you want a change in your life. With a sincere confession, you can return to your Creator and He will reveal Himself to you as you pray this prayer in the sincerity of your heart:

Father, I come to You realizing that You are God and that You will meet those who diligently seek You. I come seeking the truth. The truth lies with You and You alone. I give You my heart and yield my life to You through faith in Jesus Christ, who gave His life for me. I receive Your Holy Spirit and ask that You dwell with me always. I accept Jesus, Your Son, into my life; I accept all that He promises both now in this life and the life to come. Make Your light shine in me that others may see the good things I do and bring glory to Your name. I declare that Jesus Christ is Lord to the glory of God the Father. In Jesus' Name, Amen.

Reclaiming the Lost Gift

There is something I must address before closing this book. The message of the book is for all women, even those who find it difficult to accept. There are many reasons why this message about being a gift might create great friction within you. Whatever the reason, it has caused a disconnection from others and a disregard for the truth. It has caused pain and fear. It may simply feel as though you are lost. I may not know how you got there, but I understand why you are there.

For many years, women have been trampled under the feet of men through abuse, oppression, or discrimination. If that is you, you are like many women challenged with the idea that you are a gift to a man or a gift to others. There are many different reasons why women struggle with the idea of being a valuable gift. Through many different life situations, you may have concluded that you are not a gift.

Childhood abuse, divorce, rape, verbal abuse, and more leave an impact on our minds and spirits. Being able to work through these with healthier options can help restore your belief in your worth and value. If left undone, you can develop ways of living that give the illusion of protection but isolate you from others.

Trauma and disappointment have a way of coloring our perspectives about life, about others, and even about ourselves. Your experiences with the people in your life may have left you questioning if you have anything to give. You may value your gift but fear it will be abused or neglected. These experiences are real and have a significant impact on what you think of yourself and how you relate to others.

God Loves His Daughters!

I am sorry for the experiences you've had that created hurdles for you to receive the truth in your life. As I was once told, "God loves His daughters." He does not want you to believe that you live a secondary life. God intended great things for you just as He has for men, children, and other women. No matter how hard that may be to hear and accept, it is true. God loves you and wants you to experience joy and happiness in life.

Dealing with Yourself

What you think about yourself will determine how you feel and how you behave. Your thoughts, emotions, and feelings are all connected. Changing one can lead to a change in the other. Changing your mind about womanhood and what you think about yourself can lead to greater confidence in what God has said about you. We change our minds by challenging our thoughts, gaining new information, and giving effort to the change.

You can challenge your thoughts when you first **identify what you are saying to yourself**. If it does not match what God says about you in His Word, then it must be challenged and replaced. When you notice yourself leaning into negative thoughts or words, envision a big red STOP sign. This imagery serves as a reminder to challenge the thought that is bringing you pain and holding you back from purpose.

You can then **replace the thought with the Word of God** that highlights the truth of what God says about you and the situation. You can post this truth, recite this truth, even draw it out – whatever is needed to engage with the Scripture. As you begin to think on things that are lovely, true, and of a good report (Philippians 4:8), you will begin to feel differently and behave differently.

You cannot challenge and replace just one time and expect your self-image to change. Real change requires you to **identify and replace your thoughts continuously**. As your thoughts begin to change, you will see a difference in what you think, do, expect, and even what you will accept in your life.

Dealing with Mistreatment

If you and I have trouble finding our gifts at times, how much more will other people struggle? Please understand that although you are a gift, everyone may not treat you as a gift. If others struggle to find your value, it may simply be their loss. If you continually find yourself in the giving position and rarely in the receiving position, you will soon burn out and become frustrated with your community. As humans, we need reciprocity. In as much as we give, it is imperative that we also receive.

You cannot force others to see your value and receive your gift. But there is something you *can* do. When others mistreat you, you have three options:

1. **Continue the conversation.**
2. **Change your expectation.**
3. **Change people.**

Continue the conversation: Talk to this person and/ or organization. It could be that they did not know your expectation or did not fully understand it. Revisiting the conversation allows for a more precise understanding and clear boundaries. This is always the preferred method of responding to relationship abuse. However, life is not always so easy. In which case, you may have to resort to the next option.

Change your expectation: Sometimes, after several conversations, there remains an inability for the other person to meet the need. A person may have a deficit or simply refuse to treat you as you have requested. You must decide if the relationship is valuable enough to change what you expect from this person. You may experience disappointment in one area, but determine there are other valuable components in the relationship. The result is to change the expectation to continue relating to this person. You can enjoy this person's company but perhaps not consider them a dependable resource for you for emotional, material, or financial needs.

Change People: Sometimes, our needs are too important to go lacking. If the other person is unable or unwilling to change, you may simply need to end the relationship and find someone else to fulfill the need you may have. This is a tough decision and usually comes after several attempts at the previous two options. There are times in life when this is the best decision, and the pain associated with it produces lasting change. You will experience pain. You may also discover something within you that you may have never known you had if it were not for this decision.

Lay Down Your Burden

God encourages us to help carry the burdens of one another but to lay our burdens down for Him (and others) to carry (Matthew 11:28-29). Professional counselors have learned how to do just that—share in the burden with you. Consider reaching out to a professional counselor who shares your Christian worldview. She can help you continue to work on past trauma and change your self-image. You are beautifully and wonderfully made into a gift. You must be convinced of this truth. I strongly recommend that you seek healing for your heart and mind so that you can enjoy this life as a woman. A gift is given. A gift is valuable. No matter what, you are a gift!

Small Group Discussion Questions

I want to commend you for committing to read this book with at least one other woman. Doing so will make your experience so much richer as this, too, is the will of God that we do life together.

There are many different formats for going through this book. You could meet weekly to discuss the seven chapters. Or you could have an "I AM A GIFT" day event with reading and reflection. You could also host weekend retreats and explore the book together in two days. However you decide to meet, just stay committed and engaged with your Creator and with one another. God bless you.

Carry each other's burdens; and in this way you will fulfill the law of Christ.

Galatians 6:9

Chapter 1: How Did We Get Here?

1. Take some time to learn something new about every woman in your group.

2. What do you think about the book's cover? How do you think it relates to what we are going to experience in reading the book?

3. Share your answers to the reflection questions.

Chapter 2: How Did She Do It?

1. Why do you think the virtuous woman is depicted as an example of biblical womanhood?

2. Discuss 1 Timothy 2:9-10 within your group.

3. How can the group be a place for self-care?

4. Share your answers to the reflection questions.

Chapter 3: Created to Care

1. Grab the following Bible study items.
   a. Strong's Concordance
   b. Bible Dictionary
   c. Bible Commentary (i.e., *Matthew Henry's Complete Bible Commentary*)

2. Within your group, study the following two Scriptures using the Bible study tools mentioned above.
   a. Genesis 2:22
   b. Ps. 139:14

   Consider what God has revealed. What have you learned that has helped you see womanhood differently?

   What will you now do differently as a woman?

3. Share your answers to the reflection questions.

Chapter 4: You Are a Gift to Man

1. In what ways have you witnessed women aiding men in fulfilling God-given tasks?

2. In what ways have you helped a man fulfill his God-given tasks?

3. We talked about being a gift to "a godly" man and an "ungodly man." Compare and contrast the gift the woman brings to each type of man.

4. Read Genesis 12, 16, 18, and 21. Discuss how Sarah was a gift to Abraham while even imperfect.

   What do you think helped Abigail remain a gift to Nabal who was imperfect?

5. Share your answers to the reflection questions.

Chapter 5: You Are a Gift to Children

1. As a child of God, what are some ways He has nurtured you and aided in your self-image?

2. What do you enjoy most about children?

   In what ways do children challenge you the most?

   How do you deal with those challenges?

3. Together with your group, list ten Scriptures that identify how God sees children. After your ten, pick one that you can implement in your daily behavior toward the children you encounter.

4. Share your answers to the reflection questions with the group.

Chapter 6: You Are a Gift to the Community

1. What is your experience with women's organizations?

2. As a group, read the following Scriptures and discuss them.
    a. Titus 2:22
    b. Luke 1:36-45
    c. Ruth 1
    d. Genesis 29:16-30:24; Ruth 4:11

3. Discuss in your and experience of being in a community. Discuss and experience when you were not connected to a community.

4. Share your answers to the reflection questions with the group.

Chapter 7: What's Next?

1. In what ways has this book impacted the way you relate to others in your community?

2. If you have not begun anything different, why not?

3. Share with the group members two things you will commit to adding to your life in response to reading the book or time spent with each other. Ask one another to hold you accountable.

4. Share your answers to the reflection questions with the group.

Recommended Resources

Organization	Website
Substance Abuse and Mental Health	https://www.samhsa.gov
Rape, Abuse, Incest National Network	https://rainn.org
Pregnancy and Infant Loss Support	http://nationalshare.org
National Cancer Institute	https://www.cancer.gov
National Domestic Violence Hotline	https://www.thehotline.org
Woman's Divorce.com	https://www.womansdivorce.com
National Coalition for the Homeless	https://www.nationalhomeless.org

Suggested Reading

1. *Power and Purpose of a Woman*, Dr. Myles Monroe, Whitaker House, 2001.
2. *Lies Women Believe and the Truth that Sets Them Free*, Nancy DeMoss Wolgemuth, Moody Publishers, 2018.
3. *Becoming a Woman of Purpose*, Cynthia Heald, NavPress, 1994, 2005.
4. *12 Ways to Experience More With Your Husband,* Cindi McMenamin, Harvest House Publishers, 2018.
5. *Letting God Meet Your Emotional Needs*, Cindi McMenamin, Harvest House Publishers, 2000.
6. *When a Woman Overcomes Life's Hurts*, Cindi McMenamin, Harvest House Publishers, 2012.

Acknowledgments

These women have impacted my life either by directly teaching me or by personal observation. While this list is not exhaustive, these are the women who immediately come to mind when I think of biblical womanhood. Today I honor them by naming them and what I have learned from them:

Dr. Susan F. Wilson: *Service to others; selflessness.* My mother is always giving of herself, her time, efforts, and resources. As a child, I can remember assisting her in caring for the community. She is consistent in giving her talent and abilities to nurture others. She does so much for her community, and I often say she can do ALL things through Christ, who strengthens her (Philippians 4:13).

Cora Lee Frazier: *Always be true to yourself.* My grandmother was full of wise sayings for life. She would impart this truth throughout daily living. There was always a lesson given when spending time with her. She taught me to live with myself is to live with a clear conscience and that is priceless.

Margo Parsons: *God loves His daughters.* Elder Margo was my mentor for one year before she died. I feel so blessed that the Lord would allow her last works on earth to include me. This woman spent decades pouring into others in her home and community. She saw me and reminded me that God loves His daughters.

Abigail Citrin Kowalik: *Happiness is a choice. And then there is Swedish Fish.* Abigail was my college roommate. In all the time spent with her, I cannot remember a moment when she was unhappy. She displayed joy during life circumstances and encouraged me to do the same. And when things got hard, we ate Swedish Fish.

Jennifer Ovalles Clinch: *Trust God.* Jennie is a woman of great faith. She has always trusted her "Daddy God" to care for her. It has been awe-inspiring watching this beautiful woman overcome many life challenges and rise to declare "God is Faithful." I have also watched her defend her family from the enemy with great tenacity. She is truly a defender of the faith.

Audrey White Garner: *Trustworthiness Perseverance and Productivity.* I have known Audrey since I have known myself. She is one who can comfort and confront. She is reliable and resilient. Forever pushing forward. As a pillar in her community, my prayer is that God will grant her more than she can imagine.

Amanda Nwosu: *Whatever you do...leave a thumbprint.* Amanda can do many things. Whatever she is doing, she is leading. When Amanda touches something, you know she has been there. She leaves her signature behind and nothing is lacking.

Nicole Williams: *Faith without works is dead.* Nicole expresses her faith through community living and community service. She is dedicated to serving others and never has to be asked to do so. She is not waiting on a ministry campaign or notoriety to be a gift to others. She gives what she has until the end. May you receive the promise of the Lord in Mark 10:29-30.

Clara Warren: *Love gives.* Ms. Clara and my family connected with the birth of my son. What started as a search for a babysitter turned into finding a family. She loves and demonstrates this in her giving to my family. Every week Ms. Clara brings something for my children without fail. While the snacks are nice, the thought humbles me every time.

Glenda Humphrey: *Be immediate and direct when telling others how to treat you.* Glenda is a beautiful woman who is sure of her value and worth. She is not easily swayed by others and remains consistent in her purpose and intent. If necessary, she will remind you of her purpose and intent so that relationships can remain. She is a queen.

Notes

Chapter 1: How Did We Get Here?

1. Wikipedia. "Femicide." Updated June 27th, 2020. https://en.wikipedia.org/wiki/Femicide. (accessed July 8th, 2020).

2. Monroe, Myles. *Understanding the Power and Purpose of a Woman.* (New Kensington, PA: Whitaker House, July 9, 2001), p 255-273.

3. Biography.com Editors. "Queen Elizabeth I." https://www.biography.com/royalty/queen-elizabeth-i A&E Television Networks Originated April 27th 2017, Updated Feb 7th, 2020. (accessed June 25th, 2020).

Chapter 2: How Did She Do It?

1. Strong, James. *The New Strong's Exhaustive Concordance of the Bible: Concise Dictionary of the Words in the Hebrew Bible.* (Nashville, TN: Thomas Nelson Publishers, 1995), Page 43.

2. Strong, James. *The New Strong's Exhaustive Concordance of the Bible: Concise Dictionary of the Words in the Hebrew Bible.* (Nashville, TN: Thomas Nelson Publishers, 1995), p. 137.

3. Hummel, Charles. *Tyranny of the Urgent.* (Downers Grove, IL: InterVarsity Press, 1994).

Chapter 3: Created to Care

1. Strong, James. *The New Strong's Exhaustive Concordance of the Bible: Concise Dictionary of the Words in the Hebrew Bible.* (Nashville, TN: Thomas Nelson Publishers, 1995), Page 137.

2. www.blueletterbible.org. "Genesis 2." Matthew Henry's Commentary on the Whole Bible. (accessed Jan 10, 2020).

3. Strong, James. Woman H802 *"Ishshah" The New Strong's Exhaustive Concordance of the Bible: Concise Dictionary of the Words in the Hebrew Bible.* (Nashville, TN: Thomas Nelson Publishers, 1995), p. 14.

4. Strong, James. Helper H5826 *"Azer" The New Strong's Exhaustive Concordance of the Bible: Concise Dictionary of the Words in the Hebrew Bible.* (Nashville, TN: Thomas Nelson Publishers, 1995), p. 104.

Chapter 4: You Are a Gift To Man

1. Reilly, David. "Gender Differences in Reading, Writing, and Language Development." ResearchGate.net. https://www.researchgate.net/profile/David_Reilly2/publication/338187931_Gender_Differences_in_Reading_Writing_and_Language_Development/links/5e05b234a6fdcc283741693a/Gender-Differences-in-Reading-Writing-and-Language-Development.pdf. (accessed June 2020).

2. Bruce, Goldman. "How men's and women's brains are different." Stanford Medicine. Spring 2017. https://stanmed.stanford.edu/2017spring/how-mens-and-womens-brains-are-different.html. (accessed Jan 10th, 2020).

3. Blum, Deborah. Sex on the Brain: Biological Difference Between Men and Women. (New York, New York: Penguin Group. 1997). P.

4. Del Giudice, Marco "Gender Differences in Personality and Social Behavior." ResearchGate.net. March 2015. https://www.researchgate.net/

publication/274956064_Gender_Differences_in_Personality_and_Social_ Behavior. (accessed June 2020).

5.   Stockard, Jean. *Handbook of the Sociology of Gender*. Janet Chafetz, Saltzman. (New York, New York: Kluwer Academic / Pelnum Publishers, 1999), p. 215.

Chapter 5: You Are a Gift To Children

1.   Samman, Emma, Elizabeth Presler-Marshall, Nicola Jones. "Women's Work: Mother's, children, and the global childcare crisis." ODI.org. https://www.odi. org/sites/odi.org.uk/files/odi-assets/publications-opinion-files/10333.pdf (accessed June 20, 2020).

2.   Castro, Joseph. "How a Mother's Love Changes A Child's Brain." January 30th, 2012. LiveScience.com. https://www.livescience.com/18196-maternal-support-child-brain.html#:~:text=Nurturing%20a%20child%20 early%20in,responses%2C%20a%20new%20study%20shows. (accessed June 18, 2020).

3.   Erica Komisar. *Being There: Why Prioritizing Motherhood the First Three Years Matters*. (New York: New York, Penguin Random House, 2017), p. 4.

4.   Brigham Young University. "Mothers with high emotional, cognitive control help their children behave." Science Daily.com. https://www.sciencedaily.com/ releases/2018/05/180531114613.htm. (accessed July 2, 2020).

5.   Kamp Dush CM, Arocho R, Mernitz S, Bartholomew K (2018) "The intergenerational transmission of partnering". PLoS ONE.. https://doi.org/10.1371/ journal.pone.0205732. (accessed July 2, 2020).

Chapter 6: You Are a Gift To The Community

1.   Barcella, Laura. "According to Science Your GirlSquad Can Help you Release More Oxycotin". Healthline.com. https://www.healthline.com/health/

womens-health/benefits-of-a-girlsquad-and-female-friendships#1 (accessed July 8, 2020).

2. Mroz, Jacqueline. *Girl Talk: What Science Can Tell Us About Female Friendships.* (New York, New York: Seal Press, 2018), pgs 27-50.

About the Author

Tina Taylor grew up in South Carolina. She completed her undergraduate degree at the College of Charleston in Charleston, SC., after which she earned a Master in Christian Counseling degree and Master of Divinity degree from Oral Roberts University. Tina is a Licensed Professional Counselor (LPC) who has a passion for helping marriages and families reach their full potential and purpose. As a married mother of three young children, she values family life and seeks to promote healthy families. She completes this mission through public speaking, presenting workshops, and training for non-profit organizations and corporations. Her seminars are interactive, practical, and personal. It has been said that she turns ideas into everyday applications, empowering attendees to use the information to change their lives for the better. She currently provides online counseling. You can connect with Tina on her website: www.tinatayloronline.com

An Invitation to Write

Tina would love to hear from you about how this book has challenged your thinking, helped you view your role differently, or made a positive impact in your life and relationships. You can connect with her at admin@tinatayloronline.com

Tina would also love to speak for your group. Contact her for more details at admin@tinatayloronline.com or visit her website: www.tinatayloronline.com

Made in the USA
Columbia, SC
05 December 2021

50494929R00098